Starting with Comprehension

Reading Strategies for the Youngest Learners

Andie Cunningham

Ruth Shagoury

Stenhouse Publishers
Portland, Maine

Stenhouse Publishers
www.stenhouse.com

Credit
Page 80: "Backyard" from *Owls and Other Fantasies* by Mary Oliver. Copyright © 2003 by Mary Oliver. Reprinted by permission of Beacon Press, Boston.

Library of Congress Cataloging-in-Publication Data
Cunningham, Andie, 1963–
    Starting with comprehension : reading strategies for the youngest learners / Andie Cunningham and Ruth Shagoury.
        p. cm.
    Includes bibliographical references.
    ISBN 1-57110-396-1 (alk. paper)
    1. Reading (Early childhood)—Oregon—Portland—Case studies. 2. Reading comprehension—Oregon—Portland—Case studies. I. Shagoury, Ruth, 1950– II. Title.
LB1139.5.R43C694 2005
372.47—dc22   2004058857

Cover and interior photographs by Jim Whitney
Cover and interior design by Martha Drury

Manufactured in the United States of America on acid-free paper
12 11 10 09 08 07 06 05 04 12 11 10 9 8 7 6 5 4 3 2 1

To Alysa

And to our partners,

Laurie and Jim

Contents

A Note to Readers

This book is written by two authors: Andie Cunningham, kindergarten teacher and researcher, and Ruth Shagoury, university teacher and researcher. The text describes Andie's kindergarten classroom. Throughout it, Ruth is occasionally referred to as a participant in the class. We have chosen to write this book from the teacher perspective, using the first person singular. We hope this eliminates the awkwardness that often comes from coauthored manuscripts.

of them to come from families who are not literate. English is a second or third language for many of the families in this impoverished working-class community. Many cultures, personalities, strengths, and weaknesses come together in a new community—a community that introduces a different way of learning for most children: academic learning in the midst of a school culture.

In the last several years, more and more educators have been paying attention to comprehension instruction in the elementary grades. Teachers know that the ultimate goal of reading is to make sense of a variety of texts. Emphasizing only decoding in the early grades can lead to students parroting back text by the third and fourth grades with little understanding. Teachers also know the limitations of emphasizing phonics instruction without meaningful literacy contexts.

Recent comprehension research has brought about a sea change in the way teachers approach reading instruction in the elementary grades and beyond. The groundbreaking work of authors such as Ellin Keene and Susan Zimmermann (1997) and Stephanie Harvey and Anne Goudvis (2000) has translated complex research findings into strategies for comprehension instruction that have been adapted in classrooms across the country.

Master teachers such as Debbie Miller (2002) at the elementary level and Cris Tovani at the high school level (2000) have transformed classroom practice to focus on strategy instruction. Students explore comprehension using a range of strategies that include asking questions while reading, making inferences, synthesizing ideas, visualizing information, and making connections between texts, the world, and their lives. The point of strategy instruction is to help students see reading as a thinking process.

These changes in purpose for reading instruction have also changed the structure and tone of many literacy programs in the primary grades through high school. If you walk into classrooms in the midst of strategy instruction, you will see children marking texts with highlighters, noting important information in novels and nonfiction with sticky notes, tracking ideas with two columns of notes next to newspaper articles, and using other tools to help them note and discuss their reading processes.

Although the value of comprehension instruction is accepted in the teaching community, there is still a sense that students must have a core knowledge of letters and sounds before strategy

instruction can begin. Books about teaching reading in the primary grades emphasize almost exclusively instruction in letter-sound knowledge and alphabetic awareness. Many kindergarten, and often first-grade, classrooms have phonics instruction as the primary goal of the reading program.

A notable exception to this norm is Debbie Miller's work with first- and second-grade students. In her classic book *Reading with Meaning* (2002), Miller shows how students who are not yet fluent readers can understand and use sophisticated strategies for making meaning of texts. Building on the base of the proficient readers research (Pearson et al. 1992), Miller creates an exciting learning environment with her children that shows a new way of teaching and learning in a literate community.

Preschool and kindergarten teachers wonder how this work can be adapted when students have little or no alphabetic knowledge. More and more children come to their first formal school experiences with little background involving books and the English language.

When I first read Miller's book two years ago, I felt my excitement grow as I realized there were many ways to adapt strategy instruction for students like mine. Kindergartners and preschoolers are different from children who know how to decode texts. But these differences present exciting possibilities for adapting comprehension instruction not only to help build reading skills in young learners, but to help build a classroom community.

Marie Clay, in a recent keynote presentation at the International Reading Association, talked about the literacy transitions young children go through in their first experiences with formal schooling in any country or culture. I see many connections between her list of transitions and the challenges my students face:

A Short List of Transitions
1. Linking oral language systems to the visual code.
2. Developing knowledge of new people, cultures, and "school things."
3. Learning a working system for telling stories.
4. Learning a few features of the printed code.
5. Understanding the directional schema for print (in any language).
6. Combining knowledge of different kinds to get one solution to problems.

Clay says these transitions can take anywhere from six weeks to six months for individual children, depending upon their home experiences (Clay 2004).

Over the past two years I've learned that helping kindergartners make these literacy transitions is my most important work as a teacher. My comprehension instruction builds on Miller's work. I know the importance of helping students learn to "crack the code," but that is not the emphasis of this book. Many other teachers and researchers have written about how to assist children as they develop skills in recognizing letter-sound relationships. What was missing for me in reading these books was a description of how we first introduce children to reading as a meaning-making process, even before they have mastered the alphabet or even developed a sense of letter-sound connections.

I have learned it is never too early to start comprehension instruction. In fact, I've discovered it's essential to begin with meaning when we start formal reading instruction. Otherwise, the earliest, most crucial introductions to literacy have little or no connection to students' lives.

Building on my students' interests helps them make connections, the foundation of our work together throughout the curriculum. The owl lessons and activities I described at the start of this chapter do not take place in isolation: the children have painted what expert knowledge they bring to school, written and told stories, and read books that link what they know in life to this new-to-them academic world. These are not enrichment activities; these *are* the reading comprehension curriculum.

The Learners

So what makes this class tick? Who guides our work together? I want to introduce you to the students in my classroom: they are each unique and need what learners of all ages everywhere need. You probably have students like this, whether they're kindergartners, third graders, or even graduate students.

Bao Jun lived two-thirds of her young life in China, then moved to Portland, Oregon. On the first day of school, her mother told me, "You say, she understand. Sometime she not know word to tell." Bao Jun uses her new English in her writing and speaking

and appears to understand everything that happens in the classroom. I am sometimes surprised, though, by her confusion at some words.

Rebecca's mom came to Kindergarten Roundup the previous May stressing how hard she and Rebecca had worked to prepare for the academics of kindergarten. It seemed incredibly important to Rebecca's mother, an immigrant from East Asia, that Rebecca know letters, sounds, and numbers when she started school in this country.

Antonio is everyone's friend. He welcomes anyone who comes to the classroom with smiles and often hugs his buddies as they instigate mischief and giggle together. He helps us regularly with our Spanish and serves as a translator when we need assistance.

"Ain't I a artist?" Jake beams as he flourishes his paintbrush. Looking down at his picture, he exclaims, "It's beautiful." A glance at his neighbor Antonio's painting also brings confirmation. "Yours is beautiful, too. Are we artists or what?!" This quiet Caucasian boy whose mom worried because he had no preschool or day care experience brings great wisdom and goodwill to our work.

Atalina is a puzzle. An American Samoan whose dialect is not spoken by anyone else in the classroom, she rarely speaks. She smiles and nods, but I have many questions about what makes sense to her as she navigates our daily routine. Her silent and rare approaches to other children are met with surprise. Students often tell visitors that "Atalina doesn't talk."

"Vica—it's a good Romanian name." That's what Vica—who began the school year named Marina—tells me after a visit from a cousin when she decides to change her name. Though often shy and super-sensitive, she is bold enough to decide to change her name and bold enough to often lead the way as a reader and writer in English, her second language.

Spencer comes with 100 percent of himself 100 percent of the time to 100 percent of our learning situations. Small framed and towheaded, this Portland native helps me learn how to wait for students to think and speak about their thinking.

Kevin took time to demonstrate his kindergarten learning; it wasn't until May and June that it started to click for him. He struggled for most of the year with friendships as well as academics, but found ways to show what he knew and share it with others. Raised

by his extended Vietnamese and Caucasian families, Kevin's stories help us understand the effect of having a parent in prison.

These are just a few of the twenty-five learners in the classroom. Change in a working-class neighborhood like this one is a truth of the community, part of the oil, it seems, that makes the engine work. Students move in and out of our school; from September to December this year, for example, I have had six students move away from and four enter our class, and I am aware of two who are moving out of the district next month. It can make for challenging times.

School Environment

Our school has the highest poverty numbers in the district, with 85 percent of our students accessing free and reduced-price breakfasts and lunches. We have six half-day kindergarten classes in our 540-student K–3 school, each one with twenty to twenty-five students. Aides come to our room daily in dire emergencies. We have at least thirteen identified languages, and only two full-time, in-house translators for Spanish and Russian families. Norma and Luba are revered in this school, serving as the spoken soul between confusion and understanding for health services and daily life interactions as well as for needs here at school.

The different languages in my classroom astound many visitors and enliven our daily conversations. At any one moment, my students are thinking in possibly eight different languages: Mandarin, Cantonese, Spanish, Tarasco (a dialect from central Mexico), American Samoan, Hmong, French Creole, and English. When I realized that my students who had two languages going on in their heads were working twice as hard as I was, I decided to follow their lead and access the Spanish running around in my brain. Although my Spanish words are occasionally wrong, students and parents seem to appreciate it when I speak words that they can make sense of, too. I invite the class to use many languages when we do our daily calendar work, and I ask the parents to help me learn and write the counting numbers in their native languages. Speaking the languages of my students continues to serve as a strong catalyst for learning.

Beginnings

I started my teaching career as a physical education teacher. I began to wonder what would happen when I used the reading comprehension strategies that Ellin Keene and Susan Zimmermann (1997), Stephanie Harvey and Anne Goudvis (2000), and Debbie Miller (2002) write about within the physical movement world. I read picture books in my physical movement classes, and we used movement to explore and detail how each student's actions could help them understand the book.

My excitement for what I was learning led me to pursue and complete my reading specialist certification as part of my graduate studies. At the same time, I was fortunate to become a participant in a two-year Courage to Teach cycle, a program for personal and professional renewal based on the work of Parker Palmer (1998). I started to see students as truly learners beside me, not just as learners I taught. The Courage work allowed me to shift my focus more to the students and their needs, and away from the clutter that the teaching world is so good at creating.

After completing a master's degree, I accepted a job as a reading specialist and began working with readers in kindergarten through third grade, eventually moving to my current position as a kindergarten teacher in a half-day program.

Taped to my desk is a copy of what have become my touchstones, a set of promises I make to keep myself balanced as a teacher. To me a touchstone is a fitting metaphor; I think of a small smooth stone in my pocket that I can reach down and touch, reminding me of whom I hope to be.

I first experienced the touchstones in the Courage to Teach retreat cycle. I find myself returning to them again and again, in different aspects of my life. Using the touchstones as a frame helps me remember to allow time for reflective thinking, and to speak honestly and compassionately with students, parents, and colleagues.

Courage to Teach Touchstones
- Come with 100% of ourselves
- Presume welcome and extend welcome
- Believe that it is possible to go away more refreshed than you came

I find it helpful to turn to a different metaphor—tide pools—to examine kindergarten through a new lens, and to seek ways to frame the community and the children's learning.

Kindergartens, like tide pools, are a meeting place of two systems. The land and the sea meet at tide pools, and "organisms in tide pools must adapt to adjust to the drastic changes in environment that come with the changing of the tides each day" (Barnhart and Leon 1994, p. 7). This image reminds me of the way children must adjust to the very different environments of home and school at this cultural meeting place. Creatures thrive in different areas of the tide pools—just as the inhabitants of a kindergarten thrive in its wide range of activities.

It's easy for literacy to get swallowed into the rhythms of the day: mathematics, assessments, specials, outdoor play, assemblies, science, and health can overwhelm a half-day kindergarten schedule. And yet, the rhythms of the day, like the changing tides, are incredibly important. A publisher-designed curriculum might not connect to these students' lives at all. But our "expert tea parties," based on the children's interests and background knowledge, have helped provide a road map for the year's curriculum. The connections that the students' expertise and interest build are amazing. By studying our interests we create a community where we learn together.

A tide pool is a community exposed to change every day. The water levels ebb and flow, ritualistically, with high tide and low tide, feeling and responding to the effects of the moon. Animals who live there must be flexible and able to tolerate, even welcome, changes out of their control. They need the same type of food every day. They need similar animals around them without the threat of predators.

And what about kindergartners? They need the same type of learning tools, honor, and respect every day to thrive, to return. They need similar souls nearby, without the threat of predators. But kindergartners need different food: they need food that invites and supports their learning, and they need massive waves of time to link literacy with their lives in this new-to-them academic world.

Becoming a Community of Readers: A New Language for Learning

As the children enter my classroom the first week of school, I greet them as they come through the door: "Come on in, friend." When I gather them together in the meeting area, I say to the whole class, "Welcome, friends!" Later, when I explain daily jobs to the students, I tell them that they will all have a chance to be "friends and helpers." By the second week of school, I hear the children referring to each other in this way, saying things such as, "When friends are talking, we should listen," or "We should give friends kisses on owies to make them feel safe." Sometimes visitors to the classroom are surprised that I refer to the children as "friends"

13

Dichos

To bring the words of the children's families into the class, I wrote a letter to parents asking them to send me sayings or proverbs—what the Mexican families call *dichos*—to hang in the room. I specifically requested "sayings of respect" to post in our classroom community. Listed below are some of the sayings that grace our walls:

Haz el bien sin mirar quien. [Do well and don't look to who.]
Be nice and share.
Hay mas tiempo que vida. [There is more time than life.]
Treat others as you would like to be treated.
Xie xie. [Thank you.]
Mas vale tarde que nunca. [It's better late than never.]
May I be excused?
Tu eres lo que eres por lo que pones en tu mente. [You are what you are by what you put in your mind.]
Hoda [an Arabic word that means "morning light." When said in a greeting, it is a blessing meaning, May you be guided by the light of wisdom.]
En cada cabeza, el mundo. [In every mind, the world.]
Lo que se comienza bien, termina bien. [A good beginning means a good ending.]
An excellent Spanish/English picture book on *dichos* is *Mi Primer Libro de Dichos/My First Book of Proverbs* by Ralfka Gonzalez and Ana Ruiz.

rather than "kids," but it is part of my classroom language. One of my goals is for us all to learn about the possibilities of being friends together in our community.

The children are also aware of the language used for politeness and honoring different ideas. At open house for parents, I explain that I stress politeness and would like their help as I work with the children. Parents usually nod in approval as I tell them about using "please" and "thank you." They sometimes look a little puzzled when I add, "and *namaste*." (The Sanskrit word *namaste* means "I honor the coming and going of you" and is used in many Eastern countries.) I also use *namaste* as a closing in letters to the children or parents. The word soon becomes accepted and appreciated as the children say *namaste* to each other and even to visitors in the classroom. They have learned to show respect for each other in this way.

For us all to work together as a community, we need to have some agreements in place. Some teachers start the year with class rules; I prefer Debbie Miller's "Class Promises" (Miller 2002). We spend the first week practicing community-building games, reading simple high-interest books, drawing with new tools, and making our first attempt at creating class promises for our budding community. This is a written contract, which all of us sign (see Figure 2.1).

I often refer to the class promises over the course of the school year. When classroom issues arise, we may find that something is missing from the class promises. It's crucial that I make time in our schedule for a class meeting to use the promises we already have as a touchstone.

From the first day of school, I show I respect these children by assuming they intend to be their best selves. For example, when

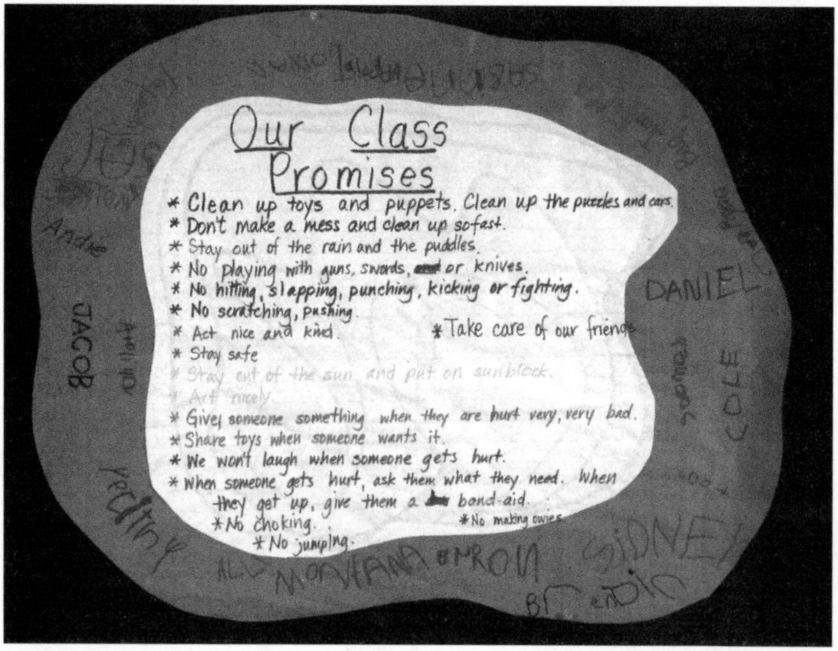

Figure 2.1 Class promises, signed by everyone.

Ja'Darius raised his hand to tell us what was scary about kindergarten, another child started to talk. I stopped him with these words: "I'll bet you didn't know Ja'Darius was going to share something. Can you listen?" Another day, I nudged the children to focus on Amanda by reminding them to "honor Amanda's thinking" while they waited for her to share her story.

When we get down to the serious business of learning to read and write, we need to be able to participate in discussions, learn to take turns, and listen to each other respectfully. Besides learning the vocabulary that helps us work as a community, our focus on "honoring the listener" also prepares children for academic learning. There are many unfamiliar terms that are part of the language of books, writing, and thinking about their thinking. These terms are central to our reading comprehension work together.

Schedules and Routines

At the beginning of the school year, I create ten to twenty minutes of time chunks in my schedule.

Figure 2.2 Leading the class in reading the schedule for the day.

For example, the first day of the school year, we worked on our calendar, played a group game, practiced ringing and responding to a chime, explored the structures at outdoor play, went to music, ate a snack, read a book, and had our first math workshop. All in two and a half hours! By November, Mondays include reading workshop, outdoor play, music, math workshop, and science workshop. These general titles are important placeholders for the students. They know what the titles mean and have a general idea of the work we will be doing under each one (see Figure 2.2).

Components of Schedule

Students are in charge of leading and reading our schedule every day.

- Lighting circle: This starts and ends our week of learning together. I am in charge of carrying, moving, and lighting the candle. A selected student tells me when the group is ready for me to light the candle. That same student is responsible for blowing out the candle when we are done. We decide the role of the lighting circle together as a class.

- Gathering circle/closing circle: These are our first and last formal gatherings as a whole class. We meet in our circle area, and all are expected to attend. Activities include reading the schedule, calendar work, reading the jobs chart, and passing out school and class information for parents.

- Calendar: Each day we focus on days, months, years, and numbers. As the year progresses, the students take responsibility for creating and teaching about their mathematical decisions involving the calendar.

- Workshop time (including reading, writing, math, science, and art): Often introduced by a five- to seven-minute mini-lesson, this involves student responses from a teacher-given prompt or direction. The prompt often stems from other work occurring at the time in the class.

- Create time: This is a time when everything in the room is open to play with.
- Outdoor play: We use this time to play outdoors in safe ways and places.
- Drumming circle: This last-day-of-the-week, last-meeting-of-the-day activity involves a congo drum, sitting in a circle, and students having the opportunity to drum their learning in front of their fellow students.

Reading Within the School Day

I love spending time with children making discoveries about reading. Instead of working from the medical model of "what's wrong with them and how can I fix the problem?" I teach young readers literacy in a way that builds on their fundamental knowledge of the world.

The structure of reading workshop is predictable yet flexible. I begin the week with a mini-lesson focused on modeling the strategy we are digging into. Usually, I choose a book that is new to the students. Before I share a book with the class, I ask myself these questions: What do my students bring to the text that makes it meaningful to them? How will they bring themselves to the text? This is a subtle but important distinction from the more traditional question, what does the curriculum say is the next step? A lot of prepackaged curriculum, even though it is carefully and thoughtfully constructed with children's best interests in mind, fails to help children connect to literacy. Another important consideration is my connection to the book. I intentionally choose books that may be simple to read, but are hard even for me to grasp readily; I want to use the strategies I ask of students when I read the book.

Reading Workshop

Monday	*Tuesday*	*Wednesday*	*Thursday, Friday*
Mini-lesson	Revisit mini-lesson	No reading	Student second
Teacher modeling	Brief review	workshop	and third tries
First read of book	Student first try		Third (or fourth) read
	Second read of book		

Reading Workshop Glossary

Mini-lessons: I give students the focus I want them to use in our reading work. Given at the beginning of our week, my mini-lessons are less than ten minutes long (not including book reading time), framed intentionally with a specific strategy as our focus. I intend to show them how the strategy helps me without overwhelming them. Materials often include the book(s) we are reading, an anchor chart, pens, and my lesson plans with one or two questions I write for the lesson.

Modeling: I use the comprehension strategy we are studying to show the students how I make sense of the text we are reading. Materials include the book we are reading and my totally engaged brain.

Anchor chart: This is a large piece of paper where we physically keep track of our thinking. I often document my thinking first (at the first mini-lesson), and students add their thinking during our subsequent meetings. Materials often include pens, large chart paper, and sticky notes.

Strategy poster: A posterboard instruction tool serves as a visual reminder of what the specific comprehension strategy is. These posters hang in the room for the rest of the year after being introduced and studied.

Practice and conferring: I confer with individual students as they use the comprehension strategy we are studying. During this time, I can identify who understands where we are going and who doesn't. I go to individuals where they are working—at tables, under tables, or on the couch—to talk with them. This is also when I document their thinking on sticky notes.

On Tuesday we revisit the mini-lesson; this time it is the children's turn to try the strategy I modeled the day before. Wednesdays are a late-start day at my school, and I am faced with the challenge of scheduling a one-and-a-half-hour day. Early on, I realized that over the course of a week, a majority of class time is spent in reading workshop. In an attempt to keep my three main workshop times (reading, writing, and math) balanced, I decided not to have reading workshop on Wednesdays.

When we return to the book on Thursday and Friday, we read the text a third—and sometimes fourth—time, using the workshop to digest the strategy more fully. Opportunities include writing, painting, watching a video, acting out pieces of the book, or extending use of the strategy into individual books.

Discovering Expertise

In their five years on this planet, these children have all become experts in parts of their lives. Early in the year I find out their expert knowledge and design our curriculum to build upon that expertise.

In September, with a goal of uncovering personal strengths as well as unearthing potential curricular directions, we launch into small-group discussions about the people who are experts in our lives and what they do that makes them experts. For example, Montana tells about gardening with his grandma; she is an expert at digging dirt. Sidney's mom is an expert at playing Barbies with her. After a discussion I send them off to paint what they are experts at.

The children gather paints, water, and watercolor paper and find places to work. They sit near each other at tables, and conversations about sharing paints mingle with shouts exclaiming how the color of the water in their cups is changing. After minutes of watching from a distance, Ruth and I gather pens and crouch near children who seem nearly finished. The children eagerly and quietly share what they have painted, or what their painting leads them to identify about themselves as experts.

Solomon sits alone. His painting includes shades of red and hints of black, and he tells me he is an expert of quiet, an entirely different image from the same boy who I have trouble getting to stop talking over me and his friends (see Figure 2.3).

Bao Jun's page is filled with carefully painted Chinese characters. She tells me she is an "expert at writing my words." She is so proud to be able to show the writing she has been practicing at home (see Figure 2.4).

When Hermilo paints a big happy face, I think he is showing he is an expert at happiness, but he insists he is *"experto de las caras."* And he *is* an expert at faces! I see him reading the faces of those around him when he has trouble with the language we are using (see Figure 2.5).

My principal, Barbara, says that asking the question, what are you an expert at? is a perfect prompt for kindergartners. She, too, expresses interest in and awe at their products, these paintings by not-yet Picassos. I tell her how we will next use tea parties, meeting with small groups of kindergartners while sharing tea and snacks, to discuss their expertise and uncover areas we will study over the course of the year.

Figure 2.3 Solomon's expert painting: "I am an expert at quiet."

Figure 2.4 Bao Jun's expert painting: "I am an expert at writing my words."

Figure 2.5 Hermilo's expert painting: *"Experto de las caras."* ("I am an expert at faces.")

I share with Barbara how I am filled with doubt, wondering what the children might say when asked to expand on their thinking. Barbara has more confidence than I do and wants me to let her know what happens in the tea parties.

"I'm worried about some of our third graders," she confesses. "They seem to be depressed about their learning. They don't think they have expert knowledge at anything." In contrast, she reports that excitement rather than depression is what she is seeing with these kindergartners.

Tea and Conversation: The Parties

A week later, I make cinnamon/orange tea and fill two water bottles with the sweet, fragrant liquid. Adding enough sugar to entice as many young tea novices as I can, I shut the lids and slip the bottles into the bag filled with two tablecloths. Later, with two tables set and cool tea poured, Ruth and I call two or three children to come have a tea party with us. At our tables we each have trail mix, plates, napkins, and a cup of tea for each participant as well as a tape recorder, ready to record conversations with our experts (see Figure 2.6).

It must be hard for the others in writers workshop to write, because at each tea party, we have several children standing by the table, listening and hoping to offer their ideas if a moment should invite such an offering.

I wonder how many had ever had tea, but I do not question how much they enjoy the tea parties. When Ryan brings his expert painting to the tea party, he surprises me again. Rather than talking about being an expert at painting, he launches into an animated description of his own bird-watching. He talks about watching them fly—and starts looking out the window as we speak, scanning the trees and sky for a familiar bird shape. Other children talk about building tree houses, or about gardens, stars, angels, quiet, making machines, and many more areas of interest and expertise. Below is a list of topics the children choose.

Figure 2.6 Children attend an expert tea party.

Yecithy	crossing the street
Christopher	painting
Atalina	colors
Brendin	T-ball; pumpkins
Byron	art; flowers
Solomon	quiet
Sidney	stars; angels
Leteshia	Barbies; animals; angels
Jordan	drawing; biking
Hermilo	faces; trees; radio
Bao Jun	Chinese writing
Montana	gardening; night sky
Cole	playing games; writing with markers
Jake	building tree houses, clubhouses, and tunnels
Sabinna	doing jobs with my mom; painting
Antonio	making machines
Daniel	making inventions; fixing things
Ryan	birds
Allison	writing and painting
Alondra	animals
Rosa	bunnies

Iliana	animals
Qrisha	ballerinas
Emma	writing and reading

Looking for a theme to tie together their interests, I separate the list of thirty-plus topics and do my best to find categories that have natural connections. For example, we could start by studying the broad topic of "the night landscape" by investigating the night sky, stars, angels, quiet, and birds. I decide to plunge in, following the children.

We kick off this big curricular focus with owls, having chosen to study the famous nighttime bird to recognize Ryan's interest in and knowledge of birds. It turns into a monthlong study of Northwest owls, using fiction and nonfiction books, owl pellets and poetry, owl calls, writing, art, video, and even a mouse hunt. With the room transformed into an owl's home, we continue our study, welcoming the other topics the children have chosen.

The expert tea parties provided the data to help me choose materials based on the children's knowledge and interests. Ryan's expert knowledge became a whole-class focus. In addition, I used the data to pick individual books that showed I understood what each child had told me in our expert tea parties.

Child	Expertise	Book Choice
Ryan	birds	*Birds' Eggs* Michael Walters and Harry Taylor
		Owl Babies Martin Waddell and Patrick Benson
Bao Jun	writing Chinese	*At the Beach* Huy Youn Lee
	characters	*The Day of Ahmed's Secret* Florence Parry Heide
Leteshia	animals	*Least Things: Poems About Small Natures* Jane Yolen
Montana	night sky	*Grandfather Twilight* Barbara Berger
	gardening	*Pumpkin Circle: The Story of a Garden* George Levens
Solomon	quiet	*A Quiet Place* Douglas Wood
Sidney	stars	*The Star People* S. D. Nelson
Daniel	inventions	*My Book of Inventions* Laura Bergen
Yecithy	crossing the street	*Officer Buckle and Gloria* Peggy Rathman
Christopher	painting	*I Am an Artist* Pat Lowry Collins
Atalina	colors	*Pie in the Sky* Lois Ehlert
Brendin	T-ball	*Trouble on the T-Ball Team* Eve Bunting
Byron	art	*The Dot* Peter Reynolds
Jordan	drawing	*Drawing Lessons from a Bear* David McPhail

Hermilo	trees	*The Growing-up Tree* Vera Rosenberry
	radio	*Radio Man/Don Radio* Arthur Dorros
Cole	playing games	*Weslandia* Paul Fleischman
Jake	tunnels	*Dig a Tunnel* Ryan Ann Hunter
Sabinna	doing jobs with my mom	*Hands of the Maya: Villagers at Work and Play* Rachel Crandell
Antonio	making machines	*Babu's Song* Stephanie Stuve-Bodeen
Allison	writing	*A Story for Bear* Dennis Haseley
Alondra	animals	*Hondo and Fabian* Peter McCarty
Rosa	bunnies	*It's Not Easy Being a Bunny* Marilyn Sadler
Iliana	animals	*Farmer McPeepers and His Missing Milk Cows* Katy Duffield
Qrisha	ballerinas	*Ballerina Girl* Kirsten Hall
Emma	reading	*Once Upon a Time* Niki Daly

Teaching How to Think About Thinking

As children start to make connections from their lives to the learning in school, they need the language to talk about their thinking processes. I remind myself to help them learn some vocabulary to talk about what is going on in their minds.

One of the first important vocabulary words we'll need for our reading discussions is "metacognition." I want them to start thinking about their thinking as well as to know when they understand and don't understand while we're reading a book. Early in the year, I wait for an opening to introduce the tough concept of "thinking about thinking."

As I read *Inch by Inch: The Gardening Song* (Mallet 1997) late in September, Allison gives me that opening. In this picture-book version of the familiar folksong, a young boy overcomes every obstacle to make his garden grow. It is our second time reading the book, and I ask the children to tell me when they don't understand something. I read the first page and pause, and Allison raises her hand.

"Andie, I heard the word 'hoe,' but I don't understand it."

"Brilliant!" I leap out of my chair. "Hold that thought, Allison!" I bring out the metacognition poster (see Figure 2.7). I

Figure 2.7 Metacognition poster.

show them the poster—written in Spanish and English—and read it to them a couple of times: "Metacognition is thinking about our thinking. *Pensando acerca de pensando.*"

"This is what Allison just did," I explain. "She knew that she didn't understand that word. That's thinking about your thinking."

We continue through the whole book, repeating the term and the definition as I ask for words or parts of the story they don't understand. This is the beginning of their metacognition work. For the rest of the year, the metacognition poster will grace our walls in the classroom, and we will return to it for support and guidance many times. With the invitation from Allison, I know they are ready. Some are in tow and some are still treading water, but all of us enter the world of bridging known with new together.

Modeling Metacognition

Reading workshop begins in earnest with a conversation about who is a good reader after our metacognition discussion. The students identify people they believe are good readers, and I record names as well as the reasons why the students believe their chosen people read well. No answer is wrong; this is their list, not mine. My job is to be the scribe. Emma tells of grandparents who read her

stories when they visit; Bao Jun says her mother can read in two languages; Daniel believes it's important to get the words right. Eventually one of the children says she knows how to read— another magical sign that shows me we are on the right path.

Sharing these inner thoughts with the whole community can be challenging. Though the children are often eager to contribute, they also tell me that sometimes when they speak in our circle, they feel as if they are on stage. I do everything in my power to break down the fear that can go with offering what one knows, but the fact is, speaking in the circle still carries risk for young learners. They need to know that when they take that risk to put their ideas into spoken words, we will more than listen. We will find a way to understand their words and represent their message.

I feel comfortable taking risks with them by modeling my own thinking in my first reading workshop mini-lesson. This year, I begin with *Leon and Bob* (James 1997), a story about a boy with an imaginary friend. In the book, Bob disappears when Leon meets and becomes friends with a human being. Although I have skimmed the book before, I have not prepared in detail the con- nections I will make in the book. I am slow and deliberate as I read the story, working hard to be aware of my own surprises. When I pause to tell them my thinking every couple of pages, I pull the open book close to my chest and look up, a set of signals I have told them to watch for.

I share my thinking with the students. I use sentences such as, "If you were in my brain, you would hear me thinking about . . ." I work to use the same words during these crucial mini-lessons so they get the idea solidly and can agree that this is important. By Thursday, I know they are ready to show their thinking on paper.

"Remember how we spent time thinking about our thinking on Monday and Tuesday? Remember how you saw me thinking, telling you what my brain was doing inside as I read the book out loud? Now you get to try it. I will read *Leon and Bob*. When I am finished, you get to draw and write your brain thoughts."

Turning the last page, I remind everyone what we will do next: "You're thinking about the book. . . . You're going to get a piece of paper to put your thinking on."

Moments later, while the children draw and write their thoughts, I circulate and confer with them, asking, "What's your brain thinking about the book?"

Montana draws the playground; Jordan draws the house. Antonio makes a careful picture of Bob and tells me, "Leon didn't got no friends." He points to the blank space next to Bob, grinning at me. "Bob is right here," he says of Leon's imaginary friend. I love having the pictures to show the extraordinary thinking going on in their minds.

Introducing Anchor Charts: "I Understand"/ "I Don't Understand" Sheets

I give them more practice the next week with a different book. *Pumpkin Circle* (Levens 1999) is a nonfiction picture book with detailed photographs and poetic text that chronicles the amazing cycle in a backyard pumpkin patch. In our second reading, I invite them to hold up one finger or two fingers for each page: one finger if they understand and two fingers if they don't (Keene and Zimmermann 1997). I take it really slowly; this is all they have to tell me—but it is a giant academic challenge to ask them to monitor their own knowing. I am asking them to think about their thinking! I am inviting them to decide whether they really understand what the pages say.

When I read the book a third time, I give them their first taste of anchor charts. They come, eager to start our reading time. I pull out *Pumpkin Circle* and we begin by taking a picture walk through the book.

Picture Walks

I save picture walks for when the students are familiar with a book (at least two read-alouds start to finish). These are the general steps I follow:

1. I hold the book up for all to see, showing four to six pages at a time without reading the words, and then close the book.
2. Each time I close the book, I invite the children to move like something in the book.
3. After I see them moving like something from the book, I call them back to me.
4. When it is almost quiet, I open more pages to continue our picture walk.
5. We repeat the pattern until we are at the end of the book.

After our picture walk, I bring the giggles and comments back to focus on me for a moment. I ask the students to stay seated but to watch what I am doing. I unroll two long panels of paper in the designated work areas, and tell them what each poster says. One is labeled "I understand" and the other "I don't understand." We read the words together. I prompt them to be sure they know which poster is to carry which thinking, and invite them to convey their thinking in pictures and words. At each poster, individuals gather around all four sides, drawing their minds' pictures on the page (see Figure 2.8).

I wander, ready to further understand their thinking by writing their words next to their pictures. I ask for clarification when I am not sure of their connections to the text, and I always write their words verbatim. Occasionally, when I know I will have a hard time remembering what connection they are making, I add my own words in parentheses.

Pictures by Sidney, Sabinna, Brendin, and Jordan all convince me that they are making connections to help them make sense of what we read together:

Figure 2.8 "I understand"/"I don't understand" anchor charts.

Sidney: "I've seen pumpkins with scary faces so I drew one.
Sabinna: "I had a pumpkin so this is my pumpkin."
Brendin: "I know pumpkins with really scary faces and gray pumpkins."
Jordan: "I know about a smiley face pumpkin."

They use words such as *know* and *had* to convince me that they are using their experiences in life to make sense of our reading. I learn a great deal about their thinking from what they *don't* know, too. Antonio draws a picture of a man picking up seeds. He tells me he doesn't understand "the man. The man picking up the seeds. I don't understand why." Antonio is completely confused about why the gardener is gathering seeds for the next growing season.

Leteshia also draws a picture of a person. She wonders about "the guy. That he's making all the pumpkins." From her words and picture, I can see that she thinks the man makes the pumpkins rather than grows them. What's amazing to me is that she is wondering how this fits with her life experience. It doesn't make sense to her so she doesn't understand. This is a crucial reading skill: to know where the reading starts to fall apart for us.

Jordan is fascinated by the seeds on the inside walls of the pumpkin. She tells me, "I didn't understand what all those seeds were doing on the pumpkin." Like Leteshia and Antonio, Jordan knows what she doesn't know (see Figure 2.9).

Yecithy's comment informs me the most. The words he says with his drawing on the "I don't understand" poster are "I don't know." Yecithy helps me most days with translating words from English to Spanish, and he knows a lot about both languages, including the meanings they both express. But what else is going on in his life? Are his frequent absences and tardies interfering with his work? What is it that he really doesn't understand? What invitation do I need to extend that will help him enter his part of the brain that doesn't understand? I get a window into their thinking,

Figure 2.9 Jordan's drawing of pumpkin seeds from the "I don't understand" chart.

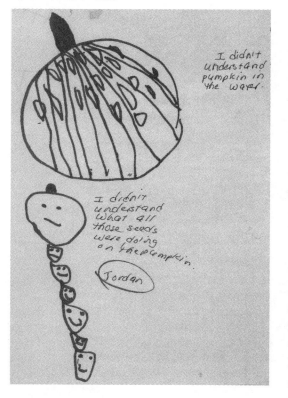

their strengths and needs, through the "I understand"/"I don't understand" sheets. And with Yecithy, I'm now aware that he's *not* knowing.

Large posters like the "I understand"/"I don't understand" sheets serve as a wonderful way to compile the thinking of the whole class into something we can have discussions about. Relying on the children to create each contribution by writing, drawing, or both is doable. Although there are times when it makes sense for me to be their recorder, I have found that student-created anchor charts put the communicating emphasis squarely on them, rather than on me as interpreter.

I also use the anchor charts to explain the progress and challenges I see with students during conferences with their parents. The parents begin to connect what happens in the classroom with what happens at home. I simply lay the charts on the floor during conference time, and the parents and I move to each one as we discuss their brilliant children.

> **Focus on Tracking Children's Thinking**
>
> Find ways that children's words can be heard by adult ears:
>
> - Write down their words on their work so that you know exactly what they said two weeks—or two months—later.
> - Record on anchor charts individual contributions to the class's knowledge.
> - Keep notes in a teaching journal to refresh your memory/write weekly "free writes"/memos/research narratives.
> - Consider audiotaping chunks of time with students. Listen to the tape on the way home to find gaps and celebrations that you hadn't heard before.

Practicing Metacognition

Besides the whole-class posters, we also work individually to be aware of metacognition. For example, when I read *The Stranger* (Van Allsburg 1986), the students draw and write their thinking on construction paper. In this story, Farmer Bailey thinks he hit a deer while driving a truck. But a man lies in the road. This "stranger" from the book's title goes home with the farmer. As Van Allsburg's book unfolds, it tells the magical story of the mysterious stranger's power over the changing seasons.

Here is what Marissa understands—and doesn't understand (Figure 2.10). "I understand when he was walking in the road and that man got him ranned over. I don't understand how he got dead and how he got up."

Figure 2.10 Marissa's drawing of what she does and doesn't understand from *The Stranger*.

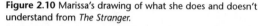

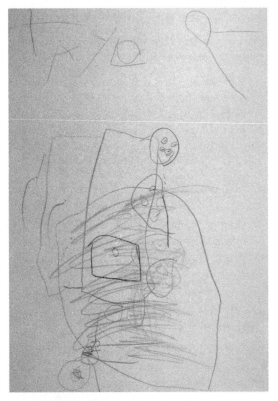

Figure 2.11 Taylor's drawing of what he does and doesn't understand from *The Stranger*.

Figure 2.12 Dylan's drawing of what he does and doesn't understand from *The Stranger*.

Taylor says, "I do understand when he saw the man lying in the road, he pushed his brakes. I not understand how he get dead in the road" (Figure 2.11).

Dylan says, "I do understand when he ran over the guy. I don't understand when the room was cold" (Figure 2.12).

The work on metacognition is a cornerstone of our strategy study, continuing to inform us over the year as we grapple with the reading strategies. Sophisticated language becomes a crucial tool for emerging readers. Of course, most parents are unfamiliar with the strategies and language we use regularly in our classroom. Although my primary role is to educate my students, a secondary challenge is quietly confirming that parents understand what I am talking about when I explain what we are doing in the classroom. Parents may not believe their children can grab onto and understand the language: trust the learner—they do.

Dylan's mom shared with me that at the beginning of the year she hadn't liked me. She thought I used too many big words, and she had no clue how the kids would understand me. She believed that until she asked Dylan if he knew what "schema" was. He said, yeah, he guessed he did. He explained that schema is "how you put yourself in the book," like the way he thought about Halloween when we read *Pumpkin Circle*.

Building a Circle of Trust

Having actions that occur regularly in the time we spend together are comforting and calming for young learners, and arguably all learners. Keeping the schedule consistent is one aspect of our daily rituals—and it is what keeps Byron, for example, sane. I also use a

Figure 2.13 Andie lights the candle to open the learning circle.

small chime in the classroom; when I strike the chime, or have the daily chime ringer do it, we all "freeze" as soon as possible. But our rituals go far beyond just the schedule and attention-getters. Some rituals I put into place, and some we create together.

Right before our two-week holiday in December last year, a student gave me a large candle. Several other children saw it and were interested in using it in the classroom. After considering how to use it, I offered the idea of an opening and closing circle to begin and end the week. We worked together to create our biweekly learning circle ritual. At the beginning of each week, we gathered in a circle (no small feat with five- and six-year-olds). One selected student sat near me as learning circle guide. The guide waited for everyone to get very quiet. She or he told me to light the candle (Figure 2.13). I pushed the lighted candle into the middle of the circle. When the guide thought the group was ready, she or he said, "Our learning circle is now open," and then blew out the candle. The process was repeated with the same guide at the end of our week, with the group again gathering in the circle, our finding silence, the guide telling me to light the candle, and the guide saying, "Our learning circle is now closed."

Our final closing circle that year, on the last day of school, was simply amazing. We followed the same pattern as always: sit, get

quiet, light the candle, say the words, close the circle. The students clapped as the candle was blown out, but then they got quiet again. They all just sat there, unlike the other days when they got up after the candle was blown out and safely stowed.

My mind started racing: How long would they sit here? How late were we for the buses? Finally one child bravely said, "Andie, I don't want to leave." Other heads nodded. I nodded, too, tears forming in my eyes. No one else spoke. I finally told them, "I don't want to leave either, but we have to. Let's go together." So with our smiles and tears, we got up.

The circle ritual helps all of us in so many ways: first, it was created mostly by the students. Each child has a set week when they are the guide. But a bigger, unexpected teaching of the circle is how to wait and listen to friends. Throughout the year the class varies between twenty and twenty-six people sitting together, yet we find consistent ways to listen to one another's thinking in our circle, whether they are speaking at the time or not. Many times when someone is ready to share and they are called on, they actually mean they are ready to think, and want us to wait for them. And we do.

One year, Dylan routinely would raise his hand, be called on, and look off into space, formulating his words as we waited patiently. Spencer waited until I called on him, put his fingers to his temples, and said loudly, "I'm thinking." When we waited long enough, most of the time he would offer new insight for us.

I model our first opening circle early in the year, and as soon as the candle is lighted, it seems the children's brains are lighted, too. This year, Allison suggested lighting the candle for people's birthdays. Sidney and Montana said we ought to go over some of the class promises. Leteshia thought we should say good morning to each other. As a group, we decided to light a candle for people's birthdays. In December, Allison told me she would be moving and asked if, on her last day, we could light the candle for her.

When Jesse arrived in our class in March, it seemed natural to ask him if he wanted us to light a candle to welcome him. His eyes wide, he said, "Yes." The ceremony continues to expand.

We come from different backgrounds and our languages are different; family conversational practices, family size, socioeconomics, and countries of origin all affect what we say and the way we say it, as well as what we hear and the sense we make of it.

Added to that is the fact that some students in my classroom have physical challenges (hearing or articulation difficulties, for example) that make it difficult to understand the words they speak. Truly listening may mean asking someone to repeat their words several times. And a speaker might need to struggle to make himself or herself understood.

The reading comprehension strategies require the reader to use their life experiences to connect with the texts we read. As we share our thinking in the circle, the need to stay focused and listen deeply to each speaker increases throughout the year. Our learning as a community depends on our finding ways to respect each other and the different worlds we come from as well as the ways we each express meaning.

Connections and Comprehension: "Sprouts Are the Same Color as Green Power Rangers"

xperiences in the past month in our classroom include multiple readings of *Pumpkin Circle* (Levens 1999), a visit to a pumpkin patch, and ongoing observations of the life and death of a pumpkin and its seed children. The children are gathered in a circle in the meeting area, discussing what they know about seeds. Their contributions are varied and unpredictable.

35

Ryan, for example, raises his hand and tells me, "The sprouts are the same color as green Power Rangers."

Ryan is telling me that green Power Rangers are important to him, and that he "knows" a lot about them. Even though the discussion is about seeds, and whether they are dead or alive, and not Power Rangers, Ryan brings his knowledge to the student-directed study on seeds. He is creating a bridge from his first five years of life outside of school to our new academic work. He is showing his ability to make those meaningful connections to the books we read: connections that start with his own knowledge. It took Ryan until the start of November to make this leap. These tentative beginnings are moments to celebrate.

Making Connections: Text-to-Self or Self-to-Text?

Keene and Zimmermann (1997) as well as Harvey and Goudvis (2000) write about the importance of children learning to use multiple comprehension strategies while reading. Teachers approach strategy instruction differently, but there is often a sense that instruction in each strategy must be equal or balanced in some way. For instance, teachers might present one strategy per month to students, or a class might study two strategies in a trimester.

Teachers often start with the strategy of making connections. This is not surprising, since reading researchers believe that schema theory, or the idea that learners must connect the new to the known, is the basis for all comprehension instruction (Tierney and Cunningham 1984). Schema theory comes to life in classrooms when students experiment with making text-to-self, text-to-text, and text-to-world connections as they read.

Typically in comprehension strategy work, educators use the term "text-to-self" to talk about how texts connect to our lives. However, it seems we miss a step when we follow this route with young learners. When I think about my students, I realize I have to start with their knowledge and make some adaptations of the ways teachers typically have students think and talk about text connections in teaching the strategy.

Emergent readers may have little or no understanding of books and stories when they are first presented in school. This is true for most of my students. So instead of helping students make text-to-self connections, I start with my students' life experiences and bring that connection to the books they read through assisting them in making self-to-text connections.

There is a not-so-subtle difference in power here. In the term "text-to-self," the assumption is that the "important stuff" is in the text and the reader has to find a way to make a bridge to that. What if we recognize that texts are more open than this? That even an emergent reader can bring her own expertise in a range of themes and details to a story?

I believe this shift in emphasis is important, especially with young learners. The children can build from their own knowledge bases, culture bases, and interest bases. Our starting point can be the children's—and their families'—strengths. I assume that children come to school with knowledge, not as blank slates waiting to be filled with teacher and academic information. All children must have their knowledge validated—-but it is particularly important when children come to school from families outside the mainstream culture.

I devote the first three months of comprehension instruction in my classroom to the strategy of making connections, because it takes so much time and practice to help students move from self-to-text to text-to-self connections. At the same time, I help my students develop an understanding of how reading involves "thinking about thinking" as we consider texts together. This understanding involves sustained work with the concept of metacognition, a process that helps us develop a language together that includes many sophisticated terms and concepts.

Schema

Now that the students are familiar with the whole idea of talking about their thinking processes, and listening to each other, I begin stressing how they can bring their expert knowledge to the books they read. And I introduce the term "schema."

Schema serves as a touchstone of our comprehension work and the way we make sense of what we study all year long. We

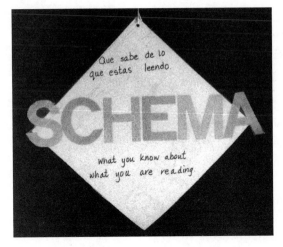

Figure 3.1 Schema poster.

don't study it and then move on. We continually spiral back to the key concept of schema, building beyond our previous understanding.

"We've been working on 'I understand,' 'I don't understand' as we read," I say. "And using metacognition when we think about our thinking. Now I have a new word: schema. Schema is the stuff already in your head. Like places you've been, food you've eaten, people you know. When you read a book and you use what's in your head to make sense of the book, you make a bridge. That's schema. Schema is what you know about what you are reading." I show them my poster and read the definition in English and Spanish (see Figure 3.1).

We talk about connections we have already made, like Ryan's Power Ranger comparison, building a foundation for understanding this important term we'll be using all year.

Making Individual Connections

During reading workshop, we gather in a circle, and I remind them of the words we have been using when we talk about reading.

"*Que sabe de lo que estas leendo?*" I ask them. "Remember schema? What do you know about what you are reading?"

This morning, I ask them to choose books for reading workshop that they know something about. What is the connection? What is their schema for that book?

As I pull up a child-sized chair to their desks, I ask the children about their connections to their books, reinforcing the term "schema" as I confer with them.

Emma has chosen *Last One in Is a Rotten Egg* (Kessler 1999). She's eager to tell me her schema for this story. "It's about swimming! And when we go on vacation, we always stay at Motel 6, 'cause they have swimming pools, and one time I was swimming and my mom told me to GET OUT OF THE POOL."

Anthony tells me that he loves boats and dinosaurs, and shows me the pictures from *Little Toot* (Gramatky 1992). "And it

kinda makes me think about this movie I saw, too . . . about a tug-boat."

Vica holds up her book *Lengthy the Dog* (Hoff 1964). She giggles at the pictures, and through a combination of gestures and words, lets me know that she has a dog with the improbable name of Mouse.

Marytey, Amanda, and Maurice also have schema for dogs, which they show me when I come to their group huddled together around two *Clifford* books (Bridwell 1985). They tell me stories about their own pets and the feats of the big red dog in the text.

The students extend their understanding of schema and these self-chosen texts by using their knowledge to connect to the books. In this situation, for these students, it's working. They are bringing themselves to the text.

Whole-Class Reinforcement of Schema

The book *Too Many Tamales* (Soto 1993) helps me reinforce how to connect what we know to what the book is about. On Christmas Eve, Maria and her extended family make tamales together. Tempted to try on her mother's ring, Maria believes she loses a family treasure in the batch of tamales. Her cousins try to help her by eating their way out of trouble, and the whole family pulls together to save the holiday celebration.

Knowing that jumping into a culturally unfamiliar book can be difficult, I show a few pictures to help the students become familiar with the story. Then, I preface the reading of the book with a discussion of things we have lost in our lives. A few children talk about objects or pets they have lost. But I notice I am having a hard time making personal connections to the book, and I sense that most of the students are as well.

Before we move on to read the book together, we draw pictures of our memories on 4-by-6-inch sticky notes and the students place their notes on a class chart for us to refer to as we continue our study of the book.

Using these memories as our frame, we launch into a reading of *Too Many Tamales*. We end reading workshop by drawing our own stories of when we lost something.

At our next reading workshop, we read the book again. First, I lay out their drawings from the previous day around the circle; we are surrounded by our schema.

"These are all of your stories of something being lost. Your schema is all around us. Are you ready to read the book again?"

After reading, I tell them about my schema, and then invite them to share their connections. Byron, our resident conversation starter, remembers losing toys when he was three. Montana, though, elevates our conversation to new heights. He shares that he lost his dog, and all of a sudden, my schema opens to the remembered experience of losing my own dog.

"Montana, thank you so much for opening my schema. You helped me remember about losing my dog, something I had forgotten about until you shared your story. Thank you!"

I am excited about making a schematic connection, and I notice hands poking up to the sky as students make bridges to their own schema. Stories of lost hamsters and details about misplaced jewelry emerge. The rhythm of our conversations shows me that the children are ready to put their connections on paper. I invite them to create large drawings of their stories.

Their drawings confirm my belief that we have shifted into deeper learning. Students tell stories through pictures: Daniel tells of losing a screw for a toy truck headlight; Ryan relives the memory of losing a ring in a swimming pool; Bao Jun expands our schema with these words: "I lose my kitty cat into this car. Then he catched it. He's living there—the neighborhood. So far away in the cottage, in China."

Brendin draws a picture of losing his hamster. "This is my hamster. I used to have one and we took it to some school. This is my bookshelf and my hamster went behind. I looked everywhere around the house." After he tells me these words to write on his drawing, he continues, "I think she was feeling the same way when she lost the ring, like when I lost my hamster."

Brendin's words are powerful to me. He is empathizing with Maria, the girl who loses the ring in *Too Many Tamales*. Bao Jun's memory is equally powerful, and I am moved that she shares a story from a country and a life so foreign to me. Though our life experiences are all different, we are able to make genuine connections to the text we are exploring together. Experiences like these remind me I am not the only one instructing or guiding this work. Their words confirm that the steps we are taking in our comprehension study are productive.

Schema and Nonfiction

Work with schema is not an isolated event. I intentionally weave a study of schema and the comprehension strategies into our daily work patterns all year long. For example, schema is at the heart of our study of owls that I described earlier (see Chapter 1). Alongside our reading literature focused on owls, the students and I dissect owl pellets, use an owl Web site to hone our knowledge of and ability to call owls, and identify our schema in many books. We even make owls out of paper bags, relying on owl books as well as videos to identify their physical patterns and characteristics. We work hard to bring what we know to each text. After stuffing the bags, stapling them shut, and painting the base coat of each owl, we are ready to uncover the details in owl-feather patterns. I already mentioned the importance of schema in our owl study. But the students help me take it a step further. Their enthusiasm and commitment to understanding owls encourages me to explore the possibilities of their connections more deeply.

Text-to-World Connections

Our study of owls is complex, and I know I need a frame that will allow everyone to be successful. As a teacher, I need to orchestrate the curriculum and split the project up into chewable bites of activity. I also struggle to find a way that students can take what they know, link it with their new knowledge, and create a document that communicates their new knowing. I realize I have to wait for them to show me they are ready for a new way to investigate text. I sense that a logical next step for these students will be the text-to-world connections. I decide to go with my intuition.

Patterns on feathers serve as a focus for our text-to-world exploration. After talking about how nonfiction texts are "true," I model with three nonfiction books what I have learned about patterns on feathers. I use sticky notes to hold my written knowledge and put the notes on our chart. The next day, I invite the children to dig through books and unearth new learning about feather patterns. I pass out the sticky notes so that they, too, can record what they notice. I ask them to place the notes on our chart. Their ideas are significantly different from mine, and I write their words

beneath their pictures. Their words inform me of their understanding, and I know I'll want to remember their ideas later.

As Byron places his note on our chart, he tells me, "The beak is black, feet is black; there's little beak spots on the feathers." His words help me see that, indeed, the shape of the spots mimics the shape of the beak.

Hermilo tells me, "*Busca en la cabeza*" (You find it [the feathers] on the head). Sidney uses letters and a word, writing the letters, A, B, D, and then the word Y, E, S. She tells me she has written, "There are stripes. Yes!" (See Figure 3.2).

Christopher says, "They get worms." A great contribution from an often silent student, Christopher's note reminds me of his global learning as well as his second language acquisition in our academic setting. With such great knowledge, I know we are ready to paint details in the feathers of our fine owls.

Our study of owls is worthy of celebration. Our class party is one way to be playful in this monthlong study, with students showing what they know through owl costumes and masks, an owl hunt (complete with student-made rats and mice), and star cookies. Our two-week winter break is looming, and instead of a holiday celebration, the students and I design the party to honor owls. The students need to act out their learning playfully. You can picture the galumphing owls in our room, swooping down to catch construction-paper mice and playfully delivering them to adults who recycle the mice back into the food chain of our owl-students.

Connections All Year Long

As we continue to work with comprehension strategies throughout the year, we'll return again and again to these experiences and the language we share around them. Terms such as "metacognition" and "schema" are no longer abstract vocabulary words, but emerging concepts for the students in my classroom. Besides the specific knowledge about things like owl feathers and seeds, the children have a more defined concept of how metacognition and schema affect our reading, and of the hard work that other reading strategies require.

Our experience with the powerful picture book *Visiting Day* (Woodson 2002) stands out in my mind. In simple words and vivid

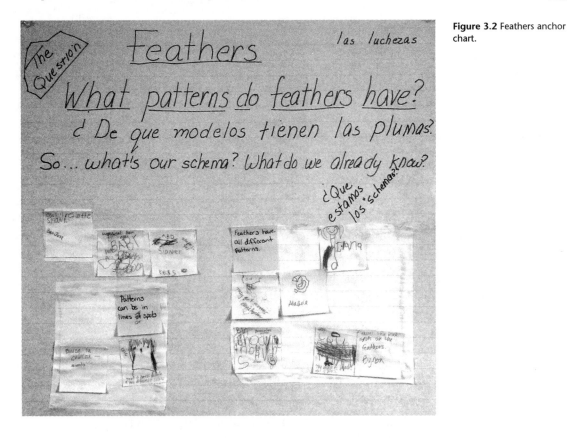

Figure 3.2 Feathers anchor chart.

pictures, *Visiting Day* tells the story of a girl preparing to make a very important visit. About halfway through the book, it becomes clear that this visit is to a state prison where her father is serving a sentence. When I came across this book in the public library, something about it grabbed me. I had never read a picture book about being in prison before and had no personal experiences to make my own connections. The nagging feeling I had in the library stayed with me as I took the book home and then brought it to school to share with students.

Never could I have predicted the conversation we had together. When I closed the book after our second read-aloud, I invited the students' responses. "What do you think the book is about, friends?" I asked. Their answers tumbled out in quick succession:

Marytey: "There's a girl learning to comb her hair."

Anthony: "The grandma's cooking chicken."

Zack: "She's going to visit her dad."

Their first responses showed their personal connections to different aspects of the book. When I asked them how their thinking changed as we read through the book, the conversation leapfrogged past a simple retelling and individual isolated responses. We created new territory, building on each other's text and world connections.

Vica thought "the girl might be mad."

Marytey finished Vica's sentence with the words "'cause her dad had to go to jail."

Kevin invited us into a world with which few of the children had personal experience when he said in a quiet voice, "I see my dad at jail."

After a pause, Emma suggested, "Maybe the man was at work."

"No, jail," Anthony insisted.

Destiny wondered, "In prison—for what?"

"I don't know," I confessed.

"He's staying in jail," Spencer told the circle, speaking slowly and confidently.

"Where in the book do you see that?" I asked, and several students responded, turning pages and pointing to pictures that gave them clues.

They continued to add comments on how their thinking changed, adding new layers to our discussion.

"First I thought that was his work," Jenny said, pointing to a page where the father is in a room waiting for his daughter.

Amanda struggled to tell where she realized that the father was, in Spencer's words, "staying in jail": "When him went in—her dad—there was a police officer."

Based on their comments, I decided to do a picture walk through the book, with a focus of looking for clues that he was in jail.

Ruth and I both found the picture of the outside of the prison, surrounded by a barbed-wire fence, to be the page where we realized "visiting day" was at a jail.

Tyler was puzzled. "I don't get where you figured it out from that," so we explained what we knew about barbed-wire fences.

Jenny pointed to the first picture of the father, dressed in prison blue jeans. "The clothes made me know." Then she added, "My dad's friend was in prison 'cause he did a bad thing."

Taylor was an advocate for the man in the story: "My dad says sometimes people are in jail for the wrong reason, and I think that happened to the man in the book."

"This is a sad book," Kevin said with quiet certainty.

I nodded. "Do you think it was harder for the man in jail or the girl?"

Kevin paused again before he spoke. "He can't even get out. And the guy gets saddest."

Several voices added to Kevin's, echoing that it is a sad book—and a hard one. The words aren't hard, we decided, but the ideas and sadness make it hard.

I was too moved to ask any more questions. Kevin's contributions to our discussion went far beyond any conversation he had participated in. Now, in addition to his sharing, he had helped us understand how substantial the effects of prison life can be, both for his dad and for himself.

Three Months of Connections

We each bring a unique understanding of life to the books we read. When we use the comprehension strategies to make connections in our classroom, the effects of our stories ripple outward. Kevin's connections to the realities of prison life dramatically opened the conversations of *Visiting Day* to others in the class. When we read *Too Many Tamales,* Montana's schema connection to his lost dog memory reminded Bao Jun of her lost pet in China. We are finding ways to build our knowledge together.

What started three months ago as individual phrases has become a communal conversation. Our rippling conversation can continue to widen as we explore new ways to comprehend the books we read.

Using Movement, Mind Pictures, and Metaphor to Comprehend

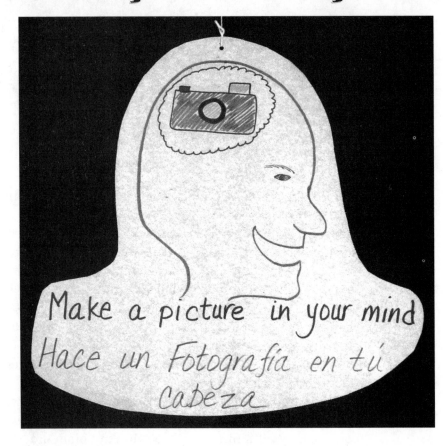

Make a picture in your mind
Hace un Fotografía en tú cabeza

L ook carefully and see which picture you'll move like when I finish our picture walk." Slowly and in silence, I turn four pages of *The Castle Builder* (Nolan 1987), a story about a boy building a castle at the beach—and how he imagines protecting the castle from the encroaching waves. "All right, now move like a piece in the book."

Figure 4.1 Being a wave while studying *The Castle Builder.*

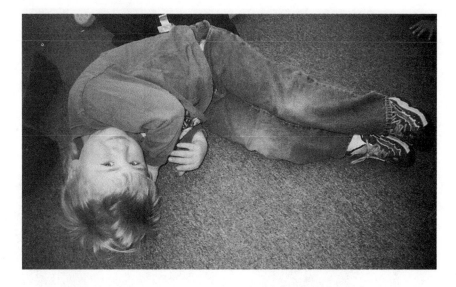

The children around me immediately get up and do just that: Marina leans over and mimes digging in the sand and building a castle. Anthony lies on the floor with his knees bent and moves them in a slow, rhythmic motion (see Figure 4.1). "I'm bein' the waves," he explains to me, and points to his legs. "There's the water." There is also quite a bit of growling and walking as children act as pirates, dragons, or the castle builder during his different adventures.

After a moment, I gather the children back at the circle and invite a sharing time. "Who'd like to stand up and show a piece of your acting?" Hands fly up, more than I've seen before during a sharing time. Ja'Darius acts out the boy picking up the toy builder; Stephen is a pirate. Maria gestures how the builder ordered, "Stop the waves!" Zack is a dragon. Shy Marina demonstrates how she built the sand castle.

Emma provides a teaching moment when she begins to act out being a mermaid princess. After she starts, she stops and looks confused. "Wait a minute, that's what my brain did . . . but that wasn't in the book."

I encourage her. "It sounds like that was your schema, from another book you read. That happens sometimes. Did it happen to you when you read it or while you were acting it out?"

"While I was acting it out." (Pause.) "Oh, I see. Thank you, Andie," she replies.

Amanda takes the acting in another fascinating direction when she stands tall and still and then announces that she is the castle.

Figure 4.2 Moving with *The Castle Builder.*

When the children realize that Marina is building the castle and Amanda *is* the castle, they spontaneously act out the scene of building the castle together, as if Marina is building Amanda (see Figure 4.2). Marina's smile lights up her face. "I like that! I'm gonna do it at home!"

The children are all eager to share their own interpretations of the book. They are connecting their schema to the story, intrigued with each other's choices, and listening intently to the words and motions of the others in their community. After hearing the book three times, the picture walk is a perfect invitation to explore more of what we understand about the book.

Comprehension Through Movement

My students don't always use drawing and writing to comprehend texts; they also benefit from using their bodies and movement to

make meaning. Many young children still struggle with speaking about what is going on in their minds. When students use movement to express ideas, we eliminate the need for fluency with words and allow them to communicate what they know using a different language.

It is my job to guide my students to find ways to help them unlock and articulate what they want to say and how they want to say it—to find a voice in our literacy work. Reading comprehension through movement is an integral part of my reading workshop.

Years ago when I was still teaching physical movement, I realized that body language is a crucial communication tool for young learners. At that time, I discovered the book *Mosaic of Thought* (Keene and Zimmermann 1997). The strategies Ellin Keene and Susan Zimmermann detail helped me discover new avenues for learning in my gymnasium-sized classroom.

I saw that for some young learners, speaking can be a tremendous challenge. In an attempt to understand those learners better, I also explored what a movement workshop might look like in physical education. Designed with intentions similar to reading and writing workshops, I connected movement with comprehension. In our twice-a-week classes, I read short picture books, then invited students to make sense of the book with their bodies and draw what was most important to them in their movements.

In the midst of my exploration with the comprehension strategies in the movement world, I had an enormous aha: I realized that students speak a language when they move. In my kindergarten classroom now, we use physical movement to make sense of what we read; it's another tool as valid as conversation, visual representation, or writing. I still see students speaking a language when they move, just as I did when I was a physical education teacher.

Here are some questions I ask myself that help me make informal assessments as students move in response to a text:

- What parts of the story are children drawn to?
- Do they understand and respond to each other's movements during sharing?
- Do they move to something in the book or something unrelated to the story?
- How does the moving seem to affect their understanding?
- Who is not moving and what is keeping them from doing so?

The Castle Builder is one example of using our bodies to make sense of text. Although I do not incorporate movement with each read-aloud, once or twice a month I offer an opportunity to move like the book. Depending on the strategy, the book we are reading, and the mood of the class, prompts might include the following: "Look carefully and see which picture you'll move like." "Move like a piece in the book." "Move to your questions about the book." "Move to the part of the book where your thinking changed."

I usually pick one prompt and use it over and over again at the beginning of the year to make sure they understand what I mean. For instance, "move like the book" was the perfect invitation for one class of students. When I said this prompt, they all stood up and moved, excited to join their experience of reading the book with moving their bodies.

I find that some students—and some classes—connect more with the movement piece than others. Some books work better than others. To find a good "movement" book, I ask myself what parts *I* would move to and how. For instance, when prereading *The Castle Builder,* I noticed a dozen ways that I would naturally move to the text. However, when prereading *The Hickory Chair* (Fraustino 2001), a book I love, I realized that moving to it would be difficult for me. It is not the quality of the story that dictates how "movable" it is. Rather, the action communicated through the story is the crucial element. When the book lends itself to physical movement *and* we are genuinely interested in the book and its message, our physical engagement is much more significant.

Mind Pictures

When we read or hear stories, we also work to be aware of and communicate the pictures that form in our minds (Keene and Zimmermann 1997). An extension of metacognition, making mind pictures challenges the learner to look inward and notice what is happening inside. Once children are aware of their mental images, they can share what they know with a larger audience.

By January, halfway through the year, students are familiar with drawing their messages. They return from their two-week winter break confident about where the classroom is and what

happens in our daily school life. I find it a good time to work with the strategy of using their mental pictures in comprehension work.

Imagine a Night, painted by Rob Gonsalves (2003), frames winter and mind pictures in an exquisitely artful way. In this book, the painter explores the magic and mystery of the world at night. His illustrations inspired the writer, Sarah L. Thomson, to write a poetic text using the frame, "Imagine a night . . ." for each painting. The children and I dig into mind pictures the same way Gonsalves does: he painted the pictures first and the text was crafted afterward.

As I share the book the first time, I model my own mind pictures. The picture of a solitary figure trudging through snow against a forest landscape holding a lantern brings back memories of another time and place. I draw a picture of myself walking in the snow and tell the children, "This picture in *Imagine a Night* reminds me of walking in the snow on a frigid Colorado night and hearing the snow squeak as I walk." I tell them a few other memories, some surprising, that the book evokes for me.

The next time I read the book, I remind them, "I've already told you some of what my brain saw. Now, as I read again, hold your thinking. You'll get to draw soon." By this time in the year, students are used to holding their thinking in their heads while I read the story again. Although they are familiar with using sticky notes, it is still a new experience for them to draw their thinking on paper and put it up for others to see.

Our first anchor chart of mind pictures shows that only three-quarters of the students draw their mental images and put them on the chart. It's obvious that some are still getting the hang of communicating what they know through drawing. For example, Sabinna tells me, "In my head I have pictures," but the drawing on her sticky note doesn't seem related to the book.

However, other students' pictures are closely linked to the text: Bao Jun's picture shows a person lying on the snow, and she adds detail through her words: "This is about that man asleep in the snow. The star kisses him so he sleep." Daniel draws a picture of the girl asleep in a sheet of snow, too. Alma, Antonio, Cole, and Montana also draw pictures that are directly related to the book. We have taken a solid first step. I can tell that the students are captivated by the book and the notion of mind pictures.

On the fourth reading, I decide not to show them the pictures. I invite them to lie down, listen, and make a thumbs-up sign when

Figure 4.3 *Imagine a Night* mind pictures.

their minds make a picture as I read. I want them to pay attention to what is in their brains. In total silence, they listen, and I see a few peeking eyes amidst the smiling faces and squirming feet as they lift their thumbs. The second anchor chart has contributions from all the students, and their pictures seem to mimic what they saw in their heads. Everyone has drawn something from the book, and many of them know the quotations from that exact page. After all the pictures are on the anchor chart, we explore together why our pictures are not the same. Their answers are simple and concise: "People are different, not the same"; and "We don't know what someone else is going to draw" (see Figure 4.3).

Leteshia's desire to be an expert on stars (see Chapter 2) helps me decide on our next book for our work with mind pictures: *The Star People* by S. D. Nelson (2003). Cloud People and Star People, according to Nelson, are "the traditional Lakota way of referring to clouds and stars. They have a living energy, just like people." In this version of the legend, Sister Girl and her brother Young Wolf are watching clouds when a prairie fire erupts. As they flee, they become lost. It is the grandmother in the form of a star who leads them home.

My intent this week will be to help them identify what happens in their minds as they read a book by noticing how our mind pictures change (Miller 2002). I start the week as usual with a mini-lesson modeling my own thinking, hoping to extend and deepen how they understand the strategy. I read the first half of the book, pause, and draw my mind picture on a sticky note: Sister Girl and Young Wolf stand scared. I place my sticky note on the left-hand side of the chart and continue reading. When I finish the book, I draw a second sticky note that details my new thinking about the many ancestors in the night sky and place it on the right–hand side of the chart.

After my mini-lesson and a day of students expressing more awareness of their mind pictures, we identify two major pictures from our minds about *The Star People*. The title of our chart reads "How Our Mind Pictures Change," with the left side holding pictures on sticky notes from the first half of the book and the right side holding pictures from the second half of the book, just as I modeled earlier in the week.

For the second read-aloud, I don't stop at a particular point midway through the book. Rather, I read the whole text, asking the children to hold two pictures in their minds: one from the first half of the book and one from the second half. After the students draw, our poster fills with the mind pictures of these brilliant thinkers.

Christopher's mind pictures are more detailed than other class work I've seen. He draws a picture of the children at the lake and the fire on the hills. He uses his pen to accentuate the children's hair and ears and even the surface of the lake. His second picture is sparse, but I notice how the stars look different from the fire. His grandmother floats above the ground (see Figures 4.4a and 4.4b).

We stop to examine what we created and talk about what's expressed on the anchor chart. Sidney confirms that her two pic-

Figure 4.4a Christopher's mind picture from the first half of *The Star People*.

Figure 4.4b Christopher's mind picture from the second half of *The Star People*.

tures are part of the book. Leteshia contributes, "There's mind pictures of the Star People."

Byron adds details from the book: "'Cause when they jump in the water, they are safe." He goes on to make an important inference. "And when their grandmother comes, they are not dead, and they dance."

Later, after the students go home, I look at the chart again. I am struck by the marked difference between the way almost all the students drew smoke from the fire in the first half of the book and the stars and nighttime sky from the second half of the book (see Figure 4.5). All but one student drew the setting, near the fire, as well as two of the important characters on the left side of the chart. On the right side of the chart, most of the students clearly focused on the interaction between the two children and the spirit guide of their grandmother. Their drawings prove to me that this is a powerful book; they are making strong connections. They show they

Figure 4.5 How Our Mind
Pictures Change chart from
The Star People.

are using the comprehension strategies. They also understand the
literary concept of setting, even though they do not use that
vocabulary.

We support our community when we use a variety of tools for
expression throughout our work together. It's important that I find
a medium to give all students a means to express their unique
voices and their understanding of our comprehension strategy
work. My job as a teacher is to help my students create bridges to
new knowing as well as find ways to express their learning. Just as
moving to books opens the door for Ja'Darius and Byron, painting
helps Ryan and Atalina communicate. Bao Jun and Jesse are writers who delight in the written word. And for Emma and Leteshia,
clay is an important expressive tool.

The bags of clay under my desk are perfect for our last day with *The Star People*. After our third read-aloud, I show the students the clay and watch their eyes get bigger. "These past few weeks we've worked on mind pictures to become better readers," I say. "You are all brilliant readers. So now, your job is to use clay to make a figure or scene from your mind."

The children go right to work. I see hands flattening and pounding, bunching and molding the lumps of clay. The low hum of quiet voices fills the air as their mind pictures take shape through the clay. Sabinna starts over and over again. When it comes time to stop our work, she is still not finished with a piece that expresses her mind pictures. Alma creates a heart out of her clay and tells me, "This is a heart." I'm confused by her creation, and I'm unable to learn from her what she knows. Hermilo's tiger seems to have little to do with the book, but our language barrier may prevent me from understanding exactly what he is thinking.

But these are the exceptions. Some of the sculptures, such as Emma's, are obviously from the book. She creates a two-dimensional picture of the brother and sister in the water with the fire flames above them. Emma tells me, "They jumped in the fire" (see Figure 4.6).

Leteshia's flattened blob of clay covers half the construction paper. It looks like she stuck her finger in the clay over and over. But her words prove that her work represents her image of the book: "These are footprints and these are the tracks for them walking in the fire" (see Figure 4.7).

Solomon's creation looks similar to Leteshia's, but represents a very different

Figure 4.6 Emma's *The Star People* mind picture: "They jumped in the fire."

Figure 4.7 Leteshia's *The Star People* mind picture: "Footprints and tracks."

part of the book: "This the part where they look in the sky. 'Don't worry.'"

Brendin uses the clay to express his idea more successfully for an audience. It's easy to make out the footprints and tracks that Brendin sees in his mind. He explains, "These are footprints wherever they went and this is the track where the grandmother took them to the village."

Sidney uses figures to represent her images: "The kids and the grandma are closing their eyes as they walk home."

Metaphor

Ordinary words convey only what we already know; it is from metaphor that we can best get hold of something fresh.
—Aristotle

Metaphors are a welcome and accessible tool for kindergartners to understand and express their thinking. One way we create metaphors in my class is using our bodies to make sense of what we read. When Anthony becomes the wave in order to understand it, or Ja'Darius moves like a dragon, they are metaphorically acting out their comprehension of aspects of the book.

Although metaphors are not usually considered a part of the preschool or early primary curriculum, they are a natural extension of the way children make sense of their world. My teaching journal is filled with references to the children's use of metaphor, often to help them explain a difficult concept. Early in the year, for example, Taylor drew a picture of a creature with spikes on its back when we were talking about what feels safe about being in kindergarten. "When I feel safe, I feel like my body is armor," he explained. Another day, Spencer made a drawing of the plants we were growing in the class, and made the delighted discovery, "The flower bud grew a smile!"

I build on the ability children have to think metaphorically. Metaphors rely on an ability to link the new with the known; they rely on our ability to use our schema. Cognitive psychologists who are studying memory processes such as George Lakoff and Mark Johnson are providing fascinating information for those of us who teach reading (Flaherty 2004). They have found that the more the

senses are involved, the more fully memory is encoded. "Metaphors enliven a text and create a sense of understanding by analogous mechanisms. By giving abstract concepts tastes, colors, smells, and emotional resonance, metaphors fix them into our minds and make us feel we understand them" (p. 230).

Metaphors can be defined broadly as "any use of a word for one thing to describe another thing." This definition includes similes and personification—all important aspects of the vivid language in high-quality literature, including picture books. The children have a chance to explore metaphor when they hear sentences such as, "The leaves began to whisper" from *Grandfather Twilight* (Berger 1984) or "Angry flames flew just over their heads" from *The Star People* (Nelson 2003).

Seasonal Metaphor Prompts

Because metaphorical language is such an important aspect of the stories my students write, and of comprehending the books they read, I make sure to focus on it. Seasonal metaphors are particularly appropriate. Children see and experience the changing seasons, and given the right prompt, they are comfortable making extensions from the natural world to themselves.

In the autumn, I invite the children to go outside with me. We gather things that have fallen to the ground as a starting point for conversations and paintings in response to the question, what's falling inside of you? I'm often surprised by the ways the children use these prompts expressively. For example, Amanda captured an aspect of loss

Seasonal Books

I look for a focus on themes that invite the students to explore and connect with the seasons. A good seasonal text is not limited to fall, winter, spring, or summer. Below are examples of themes I use for each season with a few favorite titles:

Fall: Harvesting, end of the growing cycle, preparing for winter
The Stranger (Chris Van Allsburg 1986)
Pumpkin Circle: The Story of a Garden (George Levens 1999)
Wild Child (Lynn Plourde and Greg Couch 1999)
Drawing Lessons from a Bear (David McPhail 2000)

Winter: Night and darkness, death and loss
Where Is Grandpa? (T. A. Barron and Chris Soentpiet 2001)
Winter Waits (Lynne Plourde and Greg Couch 2001)
Imagine a Night (Rob Gonsalves 2003)
The Bears' Christmas Surprise (Brun Hachler, J. Allison James, and Angela Kehlenbeck 2000)

Spring: New beginnings, growth, creativity, risk taking
Least Things: Poems About Small Natures (Jane Yolen 2003)
Spring's Sprung (Lynne Plourde and Greg Couch 2002)
The Other Way to Listen (Byrd Baylor and Peter Parnell 1997)
Inch by Inch: The Gardening Song (David Mallet 1997)

Summer: Celebrations, abundance, and scarcity
Summer's Vacation (Lynne Plourde and Greg Couch 2003)
Weslandia (Paul Fleischman 2000)
Hooray for You! A Celebration of You-Ness (Marianne Richmond 2001)
I'm in Charge of Celebrations (Byrd Baylor and Peter Parnall 1995)

with the autumn prompt when she drew her picture and explained, "I'm drawing when my mom gets mad, it makes me sad." Seasonal prompts like this help students become used to playing with metaphors as part of our work together; they also give students practice understanding their thinking.

I have used books as a springboard to explore other seasonal metaphors with children, by asking questions such as, what animal lives in you in winter? and what's growing in you? Spring inspires me to think about the prolific growth in nature, so one year, I decide to explore the theme of abundance. I know the perfect book. *The Growing-up Tree* (Rosenberry 2003) illustrates the cycles of life in a tree and a human as they grow side by side. Growth is dramatic as the boy becomes a man and the seed becomes a tree. As a reader, I love the abundant care the boy/man gives the tree and the stability the tree offers the human.

I write the terms "Abundance" and "*Copioso*" on butcher paper and the children gather in our circle and look curiously at them. I draw their attention to the chart and read slowly: "Abundance." (Pause.) "*Copioso*." (Pause.) "What's abundance?"

Everyone looks at me in silence, waiting. A few shrug to show they don't know.

I know where to find abundance on our school property. Our Global Garden was created to honor a former principal and is filled with plants from around the world.

"We're going to go outside and look for abundance in the Global Garden. *Nosotros iramos a el jardin del mundo.*" Then I repeat, "What does abundance mean? Remember learning about metacognition?" The children nod this time.

"It's thinking about thinking," Byron tells us.

"That's a hard word, a big word, and you know it now. We're going to learn another hard word today. Abundance. Ruth, when I say 'abundance,' what do you think of?"

"I think of tons and tons, so much! More than I need of something."

I add, "I picture myself playing soccer in big mud puddles. I can run and splash in all that mud and water. Abundance can look like a soccer field with lots and lots of puddles. You had an abundance of ideas. You can have an abundance of feeling for something, too, like love. We're going to go outside now and look for abundance. *En el exterior, buscaramos por copioso.*"

Today is one of those rare spring days in the Northwest when the sun is shining and the sky is a brilliant blue. Coatless, the children scatter through the garden and see evidence of abundance.

"Look at this bush." I point to a low shrub covered with tiny blue blossoms. "There's an abundance of flowers on this bush."

As they catch on to the idea, we hear cries of "Look at these colors! That's abundance." Or "*Mira*, Andie, *mira*!" as pointed fingers show a multitude of leaves, or branches, or flowers in bloom.

Figure 4.8 Alma's abundance painting: "I saw big, big, big flowers."

Bao Jun looks at one bush laden with red seedlike berries and makes a connection. "Jam," she says. "So many berries to make it. That's where shopping comes from." She concludes, "That's an abundance I never saw before!"

When we come back inside, I gather the class together to give them their brief instructions: "Where did you see and feel abundance in the Global Garden? Paint the abundance that you saw."

Bao Jun is still smiling, and asks, "Can you open some music?" The room gets quiet. Low background music plays as they paint and explain the abundance they saw.

Alma's mother recently went back to working outside the home. In the classroom, I notice Alma shadowing me more than she used to. But something magical happens for Alma on the day we search for abundance. As she describes her painting, her face lights up as she tells me the words. She says, "I saw big, big, big flowers." There is intentional and emphatic communication of her understanding—and visions—of abundance (see Figure 4.8).

Antonio never holds back. A ringleader in searching for abundance in the Global Garden, he is eager to commit his images to paper. His painting is filled with the different pictures of abundance in his mind. Pointing to each image, he explains, "Abundance from flowers and abundance from tree."

"Tell me more about where you saw the abundance," I probe.

"The tree . . . 'cause they were down on the floor. When the tree was blowing, it made abundance come down."

Figure 4.9 Hermilo's abundance painting: "*Este es una montaña.*" ("This is a mountain.")

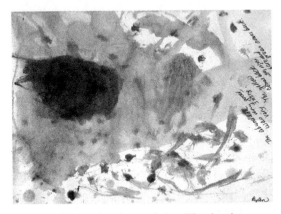

Figure 4.10 Ryan's abundance painting: "The abundance was very good, very strong."

I often have to investigate beyond the words they say to make sense of their message—for myself and for our wider audience, whoever it might be. With Hermilo, I have to spend ten minutes speaking to him in Spanish, translating the words in my brain from Spanish to English, and then figuring out how to ask him questions in Spanish so I can understand what he meant. It is worth the time.

He begins by explaining, "*Este es una montaña.*" (Pause.) "*Y un arbol. Se tombreso un niño.*" (This is a mountain and a tree. For the boy to climb.)

As he speaks, I wonder what this has to do with abundance. I know Hermilo draws and writes about trees often. I am also unclear about what the word *tombreso* means. I repeat what he has said. I remember *niño* as a significant clue and make a guess. His smile confirms I have it right. I repeat his words and remind him of our focus on abundance.

He adds, "*El arbol esta largo y la montaña tiene la silla de plantar para cultivar el arbol.*" What I understand from his words is that the mountain held the seed and grew it so the tree could grow big enough for the boy to climb it. Hermilo knows that the seed grows from the abundance of a whole mountain—in this case, a small mound of dirt in our Global Garden (see Figure 4.9).

At times, all of us are still confused by Ryan's words. Using the Global Garden to search for abundance offers Ryan a chance to connect successfully with his metaphorical thinking. Ryan hits upon an important quality of the seasons: they are cyclical. In his words, they "come back." He paints his vision of the abundance and says with conviction, "The abundance was very good, very strong. The yellow comes back. It's right here and green comes back." (See Figure 4.10.)

Bao Jun's words sum up what could be a collective definition from the children and me: "The whole garden is abundance!"

Extending Metaphorical Thinking

Not all of the metaphor prompts I use are seasonal. They also might be connected with the books we are reading or the themes we are studying. For example, when we read *Ten Oni Drummers* (Gollub 2000), a counting book about drummers keeping you safe in your dreams, I ask the children, "When do you hear drumming inside of you?"

Dylan draws a picture of himself roller skating, and explains that he hears drumming inside himself "when I'm riding my roller skates. When I fall down, but it doesn't hurt."

Destiny's picture shows her running with a big red heart inside: "I hear the drumming like it's my heart beating when I'm running."

Emma connects the drumming to her experiences at the coast. "When I'm at the ocean, I hear drumming from the ocean and it's inside of me, too."

At the beginning of one year, in an attempt to set goals for the school year, we created individual intention flags. Though some students set academic goals such as, "I want to learn to read," others, such as Felipa, wanted to "grow like a flower." The prompt seemed to invite metaphorical thinking.

Courage was an important theme one spring. We had drawn, painted, danced, sung, and written about courage when we studied "courage and community" in animals and in ourselves. Our culminating project for this investigation relied on metaphorical thinking. We created transformation masks with our regular faces

Books with a Theme of Courage

Courage (Bernard Waber 2002). "There are various kinds of courage," the text begins. In watercolor and pen-and-ink drawings with simple statements, Waber depicts various ways that children, adults, and one dog show their courage. The book celebrates the large and small ways in which people are heroic.

Hey, Little Ant (Phillip Hoose, Hannah Hoose, and Debbie Tilley 1998). This playful story conveys the serious theme of the importance of empathy and respecting all creatures and their right to live. It invites questions about peer pressure and making one's own decisions.

Red-Eyed Tree Frog (Joy Cowley and Nic Bishop 1999). Photographer Nic Bishop captures a "slice-of-life" story about a red-eyed tree frog. Joy Cowley writes the non-fiction narrative of the dangerous life the tree frog lives. The close-up photos show near encounters with predators and spark conversations about daily courageous acts in the animal world.

Oliver Finds His Way (Phyllis Root and Christopher Denise 2002). Oliver the bear cub wanders away from home as he chases an autumn leaf and finds himself lost and alone. When he realizes that crying won't get him home, he comes up with a clever plan to get back to his parents. The illustrations help show Oliver's thinking as he summons his courage.

Figure 4.11 Opening a courage mask.

Figure 4.12 The children make courage masks.

on the outside and our courageous faces on the inside (see Figures 4.11 and 4.12).

Metaphors in Community

My students encounter abstract concepts such as courage and abundance in the books we read. Metaphors serve as a tool to help us talk about and understand these complex themes. Empathy and the ability to identify with the emotions of the characters in books is another concept that may be difficult for some students to grasp. I intentionally include texts that will help them make this important link. Books give them a chance to practice understanding life situations they have not yet encountered.

In *Izzie and Skunk* (Fitzpatrick 2000), Izzie, supported by her glove puppet, Skunk, learns to challenge her many fears. Reading about Izzie invites us to talk about what it feels like to be afraid. *I Can Hear the Sun* by Patricia Polacco (1999) is a fascinating modern-day myth. We meet Stephanie Michele, who works in the park caring for the wildlife and for the homeless folks who live there. Fondo, a young boy, appears one day. Stephanie and Fondo are both sensitive to nature in a way that others can't comprehend or appreciate. This book contains layers for exploration through words, images, and bodies.

The Bears' Christmas Surprise (Hachler, James, and Kehlenbeck 2000) is an unusual holiday story. Stuffed bears embark on a secret mission to remove the Christmas gifts from under trees all over town, replacing them with notes that remind the people of those who are forgotten and alone on Christmas. Our discussions help the children connect to how lonely some people may be on Christmas, empathizing with the feelings of others.

Identifying with how others feel and react in books also helps us care for others in our classroom community and beyond. One morning, I received a phone call that one of the children, Zack, had been in a car accident and was in the hospital with a serious injury. Our book discussions had helped prepare us for the conversation we needed to have. Parker Palmer calls this empathetic stance of intentional caring "holding" each member of the community (Palmer 1998).

We met in our circle. I showed the children a picture of someone gently holding a bird in her hands. I talked about how tenderly you hold a wild bird and asked them to hold out their hands and imagine holding a bird—and to imagine being that bird held so carefully.

Making Transformation Masks

Materials: two thin white paper plates per mask, handheld hole-puncher, scissors, stapler, string or yarn, paints and/or markers

1. Cut two eyes in both paper plates. It's important that the eyes be cut in the same place so that the plates match.
2. Students paint two faces: for me, one was their self-portrait and the other was their courageous animal face. Note: Drawings must be on the back side of the plates.
3. An adult cuts the self-portrait face in half, chin to forehead, through the nose.
4. With each individual student, line up the mask faces and staple each side where the ears might be. Do not staple the top or the bottom of the masks.
5. Punch a hole on either side of the masks where the ears might be and thread the yarn through the holes so students will be able to secure the masks to their heads.
6. On the outside mask (the one cut in half) punch a hole on either side of the nose and attach a piece of yarn to each hole. Use the yarn to open and close the mask face to reveal the face underneath.

Destiny framed her explanation around what you would want that bird to understand: "You would protect it and hold it very carefully so it would know you would take care of it and never hurt it." She added that it's important to her to feel protected. She doesn't have her dad anymore, she told us. She would want to make that bird know it was okay. She would protect it.

Then I brought out a little cloth bird and asked them to hold out their hands and gently pass it around, from one person to the next. I stressed imagining it was a live bird. The children passed the bird carefully from hand to hand.

Maria giggled. I stopped and told the class that sometimes when things are new or scary, we laugh. If people wanted to leave

the circle because they weren't ready, they could. I showed again how to gently hold without poking, and asked to pass the bird around a second time.

There was complete silence and concentration. Some children looked closely at the bird as they gently held it; others barely touched it in a kind of patting gesture. Anthony, Ian, and Vica said at the end they wanted to build a nest for it and take care of it at home. Emma told me she liked holding the bird: "It felt very soft and careful."

At the end of the day, as part of closing circle, I told the children about Zack's car accident and asked the children to hold out their hands and imagine Zack as the bird they were holding. A couple of the children were a bit more literal and talked about "the bird Zack." But I am convinced they understood—and held Zack in their thoughts as gently as a wild bird. As Anthony left the class, he looked sad and told me, "I feel so bad for Zack."

We make connections from the old to the new and often rely on metaphor, one of the most magical aspects of language. Each solo voice, however it is expressed, contributes to the whole community, whether through writing, moving, drawing, sculpting clay, or drumming.

Asking Questions Together

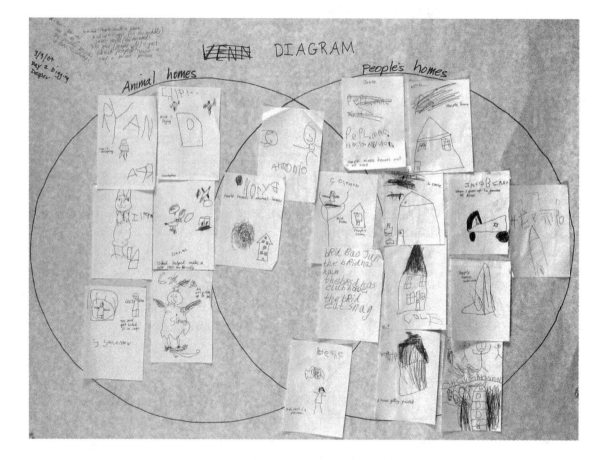

The story of a little boy on the other side of the world fills our minds today. I read *The Day of Ahmed's Secret* (Heide and Gilliland 1990) to the children, the tale of an Arabic boy with a secret to tell his parents: he has learned to write his name. I choose this book partly in response to Bao Jun's conversation early in the year at our first expert tea party. She is an expert in her

67

Chinese writing, and I want to honor the many written languages that are represented in our class.

"Your job right now," I tell the children as I close the book, "is to make a picture. Find the place where your brain goes 'Ba-boom! I know what's happening in the book.' *Busca la pagina donde la cabeza comprende el libro.*"

Their responses represent the schema they bring to the book. Montana draws a picture of Ahmed, and tells Cole, sitting next to him, "Ahmed wrote his name. I remember when I wrote my name the first time."

Antonio draws a page filled with people: "I'm drawing where he looked up at the people, saying, 'Can I come up?'"

Sidney focuses on the action in the story: "This is of him runnin' around."

I also learn about their individual reactions to the story when I ask them to use their metacognition to find the moment when their brain says, "I don't get it."

"If your brain keeps saying '*no comprendo*,' you can't make a picture, so it's important to know where your brain gets stuck."

Bao Jun raises her hand and tells us, "You know why I say, 'I don't get it'? I think the boy hungry."

Bao Jun's brain is stuck on the page where Ahmed is making stops at different stalls at the market, looking for the usual yellow cart to buy his lunch. She thinks he must be hungry, but she isn't sure what this has to do with his secret. The children pause and listen to her comment, digesting her confusion.

Byron's face reflects his frustration as he shares his comment: "I didn't understand why he showed his writing to his mom and dad."

Byron's words give me a window into the contexts around his literacy at home and at school and the schema he is drawing on. Bao Jun's wondering what Ahmed's hunger has to do with his secret is her way into the story.

We don't just study schema and metacognition in the fall months and then move on. As we progress through the school year, we continue to build our schema connections as our community grows. By the end of January, our foundation is set in place. However, we continue to practice using our schema and discuss metacognition as I introduce new comprehension strategies.

I'm never sure what the next strategy study will be until several weeks into the current study. I have to look to the students for clues. In the discussion of *The Day of Ahmed's Secret,* the third week of our study of mind pictures, Bao Jun's words show me that she might be ready to launch into a strategy that may challenge her and the other children. Byron and Bao Jun offer me hints that they may be ready to ask questions in their reading. They know when they are confused, and they can express their confusion to others.

Asking Questions

Children ask questions all the time. It's a natural human quality to ask questions about things that spark one's curiosity. The concept of questions is not new to young readers, yet I wonder why they don't naturally ask questions when we read together. Even when I prompt them to ask questions, they often make statements instead.

I know they need to be able to transfer their ability to ask questions of their world to asking questions of the texts they read. Keene and Zimmermann write that this is a common issue for struggling readers: "The research shows that children who struggle as readers tend not to ask questions at any time as they read—before, during, or after" (1997, p. 99). Knowing the potential challenges for new readers—and especially for students acquiring a second language—I want to hear them, on a regular basis, asking more questions of the books we read.

I choose a book that I think will provoke many questions. I pick Eve Bunting's *Trouble on the T-Ball Team* (1997) because Brendin, Antonio, and a slew of others are excited about being on their first T-ball team. They have just registered, and their conversations tell me they are thinking about their future sport. I keep their conversations in mind as I choose this book, a mystery about a team where everyone has "lost one" except Linda, the main character. As the story unfolds, we get clues that what the team members are all losing isn't T-ball games, but teeth. I believe it will offer frequent chances for the children to ask questions. There is an added benefit for my students who still have their baby teeth.

I introduce the new comprehension strategy by talking about how important it is for good readers to ask questions as they read.

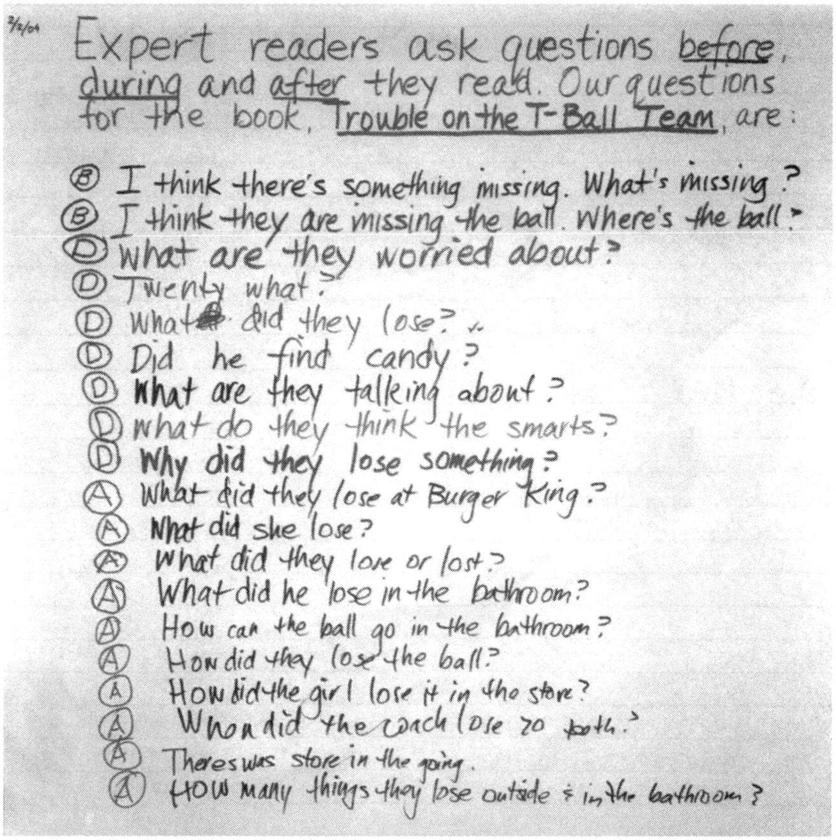

Figure 5.1 Expert readers ask questions before, during, and after they read.

Handwritten chart:

3/6/01

Expert readers ask questions before, during and after they read. Our questions for the book, Trouble on the T-Ball Team, are:

(B) I think there's something missing. What's missing?
(B) I think they are missing the ball. Where's the ball?
(D) What are they worried about?
(D) Twenty what?
(D) What did they lose?
(D) Did he find candy?
(D) What are they talking about?
(D) What do they think the smarts?
(D) Why did they lose something?
(A) What did they lose at Burger King?
(A) What did she lose?
(A) What did they lose or lost?
(A) What did he lose in the bathroom?
(A) How can the ball go in the bathroom?
(A) How did they lose the ball?
(A) How did the girl lose it in the store?
(A) Who did the coach lose 20 both?
(A) There was store in the going.
(A) How many things they lose outside & in the bathroom?

I write on chart paper, "Expert readers ask questions before, during, and after they read" (see Figure 5.1). Since this book is a mystery, I decide to restructure my modeling a little bit. This time, I show them the cover of the book and invite their questions. In the illustration, the whole team is huddled together with puzzled looks on their faces.

After many statements, together we rephrase two of them into questions. I write those two down: "I think there's something missing. What's missing?" and "I think they are missing the ball. Where's the ball?" I can tell this is going to be hard work for them—and for me.

Then, I read the book aloud, stopping after every few pages. Instead of modeling my questions, I ask for theirs. This is a long book, and it takes us more than our usual read-aloud time to find out what the mystery is all about. By the end of the day, we have nine questions on our chart.

The next day, we read the book again, and then I invite their questions to add them to our class chart. For the most part, they are asking questions rather than making statements. Ironically, their questions show me that they have no idea what this book is about. "What did he lose in the bathroom?" "How can a ball go in the bathroom?" "When did the coach lose twenty teeth?" They are only beginning to understand that the central mystery is connected to losing teeth.

For our third day, I decide to include movement to help them talk about their questions. I summarize the first part of the book, then read aloud the rest. "Your job, friends," I tell them, "is to take your question and figure out how to move to your question. How can you ask your question with your body?"

An innocent bystander might believe these moving bodies are simply free-dancing. However, when they explain the questions they have been moving to, they are indeed related to their first set of questions we have listed on the chart paper. Sidney moves to the yellow dog high-fiving for her question, "What's next after the dog high-fives the guy?"

Montana and Cole shrug together to ask, "How did the coach lose twenty teeth?"

Unfortunately, they are no closer to understanding the book. Neither of the themes that I thought would capture their attention—T-ball and children losing baby teeth—really ignited questioning strategies in these readers.

I know that for our next week's study, I need to find a catalyst for summoning the questioning brilliance that they use so frequently in their everyday lives, but rarely in relation to the books. I decide to try a different medium, and because I am awed by the movie myself, I consider using *Winged Migration* (2003). This amazing documentary details the annual migrations of birds around the world. The audience sees the nesting rituals and remote homelands of dozens of types of migrating birds. The sound track of music from around the world echoes the majesty and danger of the birds' endless flight.

Having seen this film with my five-year-old daughter and heard her barrage of questions, I wonder what the children will make of it. I wonder if we can practice the questioning strategy while immersing ourselves in the lives of birds again, this time from a documentary angle.

In addition, Hermilo wants to become an expert on radios, and I could show the special footage on the DVD of how the film crew uses recording equipment to document the sound and lives of the birds in their migrations as a link to his interest.

First Viewing–*Winged Migration*

The sounds of the first song from the *Winged Migration* sound track fill the silences in our room. Soft chatter can be heard among the children as they wonder what the music is about, and what the sounds might be from. After a minute or so, I pause the music, hoping they want to know more. I am rewarded with an enthusiastic yes in the form of their responses and questions, such as, "I heard birds!" and "What's that weird music?"

A lot of thought goes into my preparation for using film excerpts. I ask the same questions in any media I choose to use. How will this "text" deepen their understanding and ability to use the comprehension strategy? How will it connect to the schema of each learner? How much time do I need to dedicate for this excerpt? Will it sustain their interest in a positive and evocative way? How much time will we need to unpack the learning?

As I previewed the movie at home, I searched for three twenty-minute chunks that would entice students to ask amazing questions. I watched with my five-year-old daughter, my resident assessor of multimedia material for kindergarten. I chose parts that amazed Alysa and me: birds reacting to seasonal challenges, flamboyant dancing and ritual behavior, and action footage that captured the perils of winged animals' lives. Alysa and I also decided together what wouldn't be appropriate. For example, the scene of the crab consuming the hatchling would not be an ideal segment.

Of course, I had to consider the time available in my class as well as the comprehension strategy that we were studying. One of the segments was twenty minutes long, but for the other two days, I decided to use several short segments that when combined lasted about twenty minutes.

We've studied birds. It's a familiar world to my students. When I turn on the DVD, they're eager to see where the movie will take them. Rosa moves front and center, two feet from the DVD stand, a smile on her face and attention fixed on the screen. The children

become engaged with the sequence of a boy releasing a trapped bird, and their voices call out.

I realize minutes into this segment that I can hear them asking questions. Cole asks, "Why can't they fly away?"

Sidney whispers, "Why are those birds moving like that?"

Byron wonders, "What are they doing?"

I smile, my eyes moving back and forth from students to the screen, listening to their questions and believing we have turned a corner. I stop the DVD after our twenty-minute viewing. I ask, "What are your questions?"

Ryan says, "The goose, it was lost. . . . He was sad." He retells part of the movie, then asks, "Does the goose find his friends?"

Jake contributes, "The goose almost snowed down. Did they fall down the mountain?"

This reading workshop time doesn't provide me with many answers about teaching the questioning strategy; rather, I am bombarded with my own questions. What makes the concept of asking a question so difficult for five- and six-year-olds? What helps the children ask genuine questions of this "text"? Is it that they have a significant schema built up on birds? Is it the different medium? I know that although we made a valiant attempt at asking questions in response to a book last week, it didn't work.

Yet now, days later, the children are asking questions before, during, and after the movie. I'm glad I'm asking questions I don't know the answers to, and I realize that for the first time in this strategy, the students and I are working hard to make sense of what we know.

By the time we have seen the last chunk of the movie, the students are asking powerful questions, and they are passionately involved. During the rain-forest scene where a boat carries caged animals down a river, the children get very quiet. Then I hear Ryan asking the question that many students may have been wondering. "It's sad. Why don't they let them out? They're sad, Andie."

He tells the bird on the screen, "That's the way out" as it figures out how to open its cage and fly away. Ryan claps his approval of the bird's escape.

After the movie, Cole, Sidney, Sabinna, and Daniel all ask questions about how the bird got out of its cage. Byron also thinks about the bird's escape, but his question is different: "When the bird got out of his cage, there was a big sound. What was the sound?"

Figure 5.2 Children work on the "How?" anchor chart for *Winged Migration.*

Ryan brings up a question I had never thought about. In one scene, the adult penguins huddle around an egg, then a penguin chick, serving as protectors. Ryan wonders, "The penguins jump. How do the bodies form a circle?"

I am hopeful we can capture their questions to create our next text for the class to read together. I have three six-foot-long sheets of butcher paper, each labeled with a different questioning start: "How?" "Why?" and "What?"

I explain to the children what the posters say and invite them to draw and write their biggest question from the movie on the appropriate poster. As Ruth and I watch, the children create pictures that are full of details and colors. We write their questions next to their pictures, documenting their thinking in their own words (see Figures 5.2 and 5.3).

Of course, some of the questions recorded on the large sheets have already been asked, such as Leteshia's. Next to her picture, we record her words: "The kid on the first day, the picture that freed the bird—I want to know how he freed the bird." She's held that question for three days, since our discussion of the opening scene. Cole asked a similar question during the movie, in wondering, "Why can't they fly away?" But Cole's question has changed. Now he wonders, "How did the bird get out of the cage?" Many class-mates ask the same question.

Figure 5.3 Andie helps children write on the "I wonder what" chart for *Winged Migration.*

The questions the students asked before and after the first day's film segment were all "closed" questions: ones that could be answered by a yes or a no. By day two, questions start with words such as, "Why?" "Where?" "How?" By the time the students put their questions down on paper, they are no longer confined to literal yes/no questions; rather, they are eager to explore more open questions.

I see examples of this from Rosa, who asks, *"Quien habla?"* (Who is speaking?) No one else—me included—had wondered out loud who the narrator was. Byron makes an interesting link to the rain forest with his question, "The bird tries to fly through stormy rain like a butterfly. How do they fly different?" Hermilo takes my thinking to a whole new level by comparing the wings of a bird to the headset for a telephone: *"Como estas su salas como uno telefono?"*

Through this project, I hear the voices of my English language learners rise up. All of a sudden, language is not a limitation for any of us, either in the delivery of the text or in the communication of what they understand or wonder about. Although I can speak some Spanish, I am no longer the primary voice who translates and speaks for Rosa, Hermilo, and Iliana.

Because this documentary does not rely on spoken words and because we returned to the text again and again, language was no

longer a limitation in our classroom. We extended the time we spent on the text and opened up different ways to express questions through drawing, moving, writing, and talking. What worked for the English language learners worked for the native English speakers.

Questioning More Deeply

To take our questioning deeper, I decide to help the students investigate how we can mark our confusions in the text. During the Monday morning mini-lesson on the first day of learning about ways for marking confusion, I read the book *In English, of Course* (Nobisso 2002). Set in the Bronx during the 1950s, this story tells of the linguistic misunderstandings that happen during Josephine's first day of school.

A newcomer from Italy, Josephine has lived in the city long enough to have learned a few words in English, but is overcome when her teacher makes her stand up in front of the class and tell about her life in Italy—in English, of course. The result is a tale of adventures and multicultural miscommunications as Josephine attempts to make herself understood.

I am familiar with the book but haven't read it carefully, and the connections I share are genuine and spontaneous. I write the quotation that caused me to stumble and what I think it means on sticky notes and put both on the chart paper I prepared before class started. The chart is set up in two columns with space for the quotation in one column and my thinking in the other. The students know that their turn to use strategies to make sense of the text comes tomorrow and in the subsequent workshops this week.

The next day, we take a look at the strategy poster again. I invite them to enter my thinking from Monday, and we look again at my start on the anchor chart. At this point, it's tempting for me to just tell them what we'll be doing with our thinking after we read.

But when I do, I realize I am talking too much and they aren't ready to remember the prompt. So instead, I invite them to hold their thinking in their minds using the strategy we are working on. I ask them to remember when their thinking falls apart. "What words or

quotes confuse you?" I ask. "Does this sound like a word? Does this make sense?"

After reading through the whole book one time, we take a picture walk of the book, page by page. Now I ask, "Tell me when you didn't understand the words." When Cole raises his hand, he helps me find the exact quotation that confuses him: "Juan, speak to us of Puerto Rico." I write it on the chart paper.

I ask who else is confused by this quotation and write the names of all the children who share Cole's confusion under the quotation on the chart paper. Atalina is confused by the sentence, "That was just the word she was looking for," and I write it down along with all the names of those who tell me that that is where they didn't understand the words.

I invite them to draw their thinking about their quotation on large sticky notes. With their pictures finished and their names on their sticky notes, they fill in the poster, so that we now have a list of both their confusions and what they think those words might mean (see Figure 5.4).

Jordan draws a girl with a magnifying glass in her hand as she struggles to make sense of the words in the book: "Josephine clearly saw the memory" (see Figure 5.5). Solomon chooses the words, "Juan, speak to us of Puerto Rico." On this page of the book, Juan relies on a world globe to tell of his homeland. Solomon isn't sure how this "circle" could help explain Juan's home. His sticky note drawing is of a wide-eyed Juan, and he tells me, "I still . . . got the circle" (see Figure 5.6).

I also learn about misunderstandings that come from simple words in the text

Figure 5.4 Anchor chart for *In English, of Course.*

Figure 5.5 Jordan's sticky note.

Figure 5.6 Solomon's sticky note.

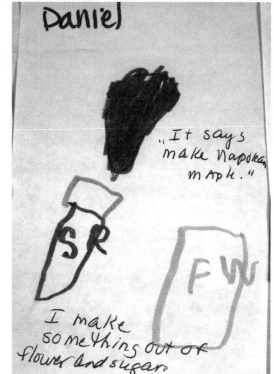

Figure 5.7 Daniel's sticky note.

that can have more than one meaning. The verb "made" leads more than one student astray. In the story, Josephine realizes she used the word "Napoli" rather than Naples when she spoke about the city where she was born. She tells herself that next time, she will use the English name for the city and "Make Napoli, Naples." Several children are confused by what "make" could mean on this page. Daniel draws a container of sugar, labeled "SR," and one of flour, with the letters "FW." "I make something out of flour and sugar," he tells me, looking puzzled (see Figure 5.7). Byron shares his confusion. For the same quotation, he decides, "It probably means, 'Make hearts for your friends.'"

The children teach me that their metacognition skills are growing: they can pinpoint where in the book they are confused. And, equally important, they are willing to show their attempts to understand their classmates' thinking.

Webs in Kindergarten

At the start of the year, the students signed their names under one half of a sign-in sentence (see Figure 5.8). For example, one day I headed one side with the sentence "I like apples" and the other side "I like oranges." Each day, I changed the categories to give the children practice reading sight words and familiar text.

Midway through the year, I noticed that students were signing their names on both halves of the page, and they informed me that their names belonged in both places. The birth of Venn diagrams had occurred in our room. The partially overlapping circle on our new sign-in sheet holds three places for names. For students to sign in, they need to decide how to answer the question for themselves. For example, one day's sign-in sheet might read: "I like cookies" and "I like ice cream." The middle space isn't labeled; the students know this is the place to sign in if they like both (see Figure 5.9).

Figure 5.8 The original sign-in survey.

Figure 5.9 Children use the Venn diagram survey.

For a number of weeks, I created sign-in sheets using Venn diagrams. The students showed me they were savvy at the Venn diagram sign-in sheets; it seemed they were inviting me to consider introducing a more difficult way to document thinking. It was their confidence that nudged me into the kindergarten world of webs.

I had never used a web structure with kindergartners, believing it was for more academically experienced students. I wanted to see what would happen when students were invited to use webs to document their new understanding of texts.

I had never considered using adult poetry with my students, but "Backyard" by Mary Oliver (2003) seemed like it might serve as a natural next step with our work in digging deeper.

Backyard
I had no time to haul out all
the dead stuff so it hung, limp
or dry, wherever the wind swung it

over or down or across. All summer
it stayed that way, untrimmed, and
thickened. The paths grew
damp and uncomfortable and mossy until
nobody could get through but a mouse or a

shadow. Blackberries, ferns, leaves, litter
totally without direction management
supervision. The birds loved it.

We read "Backyard" the week before spring break. When the students are ready, I tell them we are going to take another look at how animals build their homes. I read the poem and model my connections as I dig more deeply into this poem.

Centered on the chart paper, I have written the word "Nests" with a circle around it (see Figure 5.10). I choose phrases that open my thinking to new understandings about yard debris and how birds use waste for nests. I write the phrases on sticky notes and place them on our large chart paper.

With simple eloquence, Mary Oliver creates an incredible portrait of her overgrown backyard. I can see the children are eager to draw what they are seeing in their minds as well.

With sticky notes and good pens in hand, students start to create pictures evoked by the poem. When they are finished, they place their sticky notes on the chart. There is no set place on the chart for their notes today; it seems more important to be sure they find a way to document their thinking.

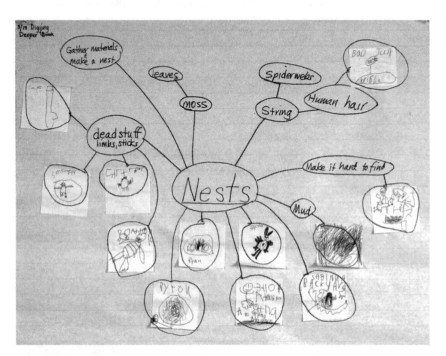

Figure 5.10 The web response to Mary Oliver's "Backyard."

The next day, I read the poem again. Returning to the poem is fascinating. After I read it, they act it out using movement; they are sticks, dead branches, birds, litter. They are living the poem.

Jake notices that we did not finish our chart. He seems to know that we have more work to do, and he is right. I have a hard time quelling my excitement, and I am again reminded of how surprises in the classroom are actually assessments in action. I confirm how right Jake is and inform the children that we need to rearrange our sticky notes to connect our ideas. I start by reading the labels, inviting the children to decide where their sticky note goes and what label it ought to be connected with. Again, as on many of our previous charts, the only right answer is theirs, and I am careful to keep my judgments and categories silent. Children help me to realign their sticky notes, and I draw lines from the labels I wrote yesterday to their notes.

Daniel's voice calls out from the group, telling me he wants to add something to our chart. Other students also remember something important that they didn't write about yesterday. "You're right," I tell Daniel, "and I imagine you are not the only one who wants to add to this chart. We could add our new learning about nests forever. But let's do something else. It is time for you to create your own web."

I hold up a large piece of white construction paper, blank except for the word "Nests" in the middle with a circle around it. "You have your own paper that says 'Nests' on it, and your job is to make sure that your pictures and words show what's important for nests. You can use books for more information."

Our city library offers a search service for educators seeking books on specific topics. They collect and reserve large quantities of materials. These are just four of the forty books that I was able to check out. Check with your local library system to see if you have a similar supportive service.

Eyewitness Explorers: Birds by Jill Bailey and David Burnie (1997)
Owl Babies by Martin Waddell and Patrick Benson (1996)
What Do You Do with a Tail Like This? by Robin Page and Steve Jenkins (2003)
Animal Encyclopedia by Dorling-Kindersley Publishing (2000)

After the children get the materials they need and start working, I step back and watch for a while. I am surprised and excited about how they seem to know to go right to work. Their knowledge—and their schema—informs them. And they are able to work independently.

Figure 5.11 Sabinna's nest web.

Sabinna gets herself settled under a table. She has all her tools with her, and she works the entire twenty-five minutes without interacting with anyone else. She ends up with a drawing, a story, and a web (see Figure 5.11). Sabinna knows her ideas go in the web circles, so she writes letters in those circles to represent her ideas. Then, she puts all her important information in her picture, not in the web itself as we had done as a class.

Figure 5.12 Byron's nest web.

This tells me that we have an important bridge to build tomorrow. It will be a time to identify what the circles are for. For Sabinna and others, it is a leap from drawing what they know in a picture to drawing in a web format.

But other children, such as Byron, understand the concept. He keeps saying his thoughts are bursting out of his head. When he sits down to do his work, he is very purposeful. In his web, he has lots of lines coming out of the center circle, with a place for a spiderweb, an eagle claw, and more. I don't know what all the pictures in his web represent, but what's amazing to me is that he is so clear on the concept. All the circles represent what's important when he thinks about what he knows of nests (see Figure 5.12).

At first, Cole doesn't understand making a web. He and Montana know it is supposed to be about birds, but they can't figure out how to build the web. Cole had several pictures started. Then he and Montana flipped their papers over, and now they are doing a whole big story about King Kong. I am confused by their work and ask them, "Who is King Kong?"

Thank goodness I asked! King Kong is the name of their eagle, the model bird whose nest they are creating, not King Kong the

Figure 5.13 Cole's nest web.

giant ape I was imagining. Because we have read about how birds use hair in their nests, Cole is drawing hair for a wig for his bald eagle, King Kong (so that he will have hair). He adds mud and sticks. When he runs out of things to add, he comes to me and says he is finished.

I send him back to the books and he locates an interesting addition. When he finds a book on penguins in their habitat, he writes the word "krill" for the food they might bring to their nests. He doesn't usually write words, but today he copies the word on his web and circles it, then draws a line to the center "Nests" circle (see Figure 5.13).

It's obvious that our work with webs is only beginning; we still have more to do. Cole knows the words are important. He knows what he is looking for, and he knows he can use books to confirm his search. He helps lead me to the next strategy we will explore together: What's important on the page? How can we determine importance? I know webs can continue to play a crucial role in our reading workshop.

Questioning Texts and Our Community

Teaching comprehension strategies doesn't happen in isolation; classroom dynamics continue to play out. I am reminded annually of the struggles I experience with kindergartners as we hit midyear. A colleague once told me, "When you tell a student a thousand times to do something, who's the slow learner?"

It is a windy Thursday morning and we are still asking questions in literature. The blustery air outside seems to come through our windows, and many children are talking too loudly for us to focus in the circle.

I find myself repeating my words over and over: "Can you say that again? I didn't hear your words." "Thank you, Emma and Byron, for pointing your knees toward Jordan and waiting for her

The Clip System

Although much of my classroom revolves around student choice, I know I have to serve as the safety and behavior gatekeeper. In searching for a tool that seemed fair and also placed responsibility in the hands of students, I found this clothespin system from a teacher friend. It works with mostly successful moments and often, the student is in charge of the actions connected to it (see Figure 5.14).

- A sheet of 5-by-18-inch posterboard serves as the base. At least half of the sheet is colored green. The green section is where all clothespins start every day, no matter what. The rest of the sheet is separated into three equal parts: yellow, red, and white.
- Each student has a clothespin with his or her name written on both sides. I like to make sure the name reads right side up no matter what side of the clothespin is facing out.
- Students hold primary responsibility for moving clips during the day.
- When students break a class promise or act in an unsafe manner, I ask them what they want to change about what they are doing. I often use the words, "What's your problem?" and "How are you going to fix it?"
- If the unsafe action continues, I tell them, "That [or I name the behavior] is yellow behavior. Please move your clip." If the children continue to be unsafe, I tell them, "That is red behavior. Please move your clip to red."
- During the first part of the school year, I allow students to physically change their behavior and then when consistent, to move their clip back to the color above

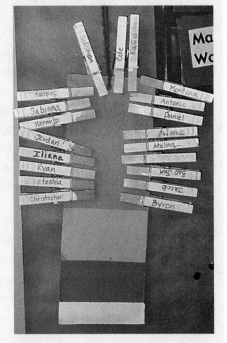

Figure 5.14 The clip system.

where their clip is. For example, if a student's clip is in yellow, and he or she has worked to correct a broken promise or behavior, I ask if he or she is ready to return the clip to green.
- Much like the "three strikes and you're out" idea, continued unsafe behavior means they need to move their clip to white. The white area on the board is reserved for serious infractions, always when students have already had their clip in yellow and then red spaces. White behavior is irrevocable, and once the clip is in white, it stays there. It means I will contact the student's parents that day. In my contact, I explain the system and the challenges their child was having, but I also encourage them to problem solve with their son or daughter.
- I am responsible for moving all clips to green before class starts each morning. I also am responsible for enforcing the system fairly. When I consistently give one child a break, others notice my unfairness. However, young learners also mysteriously realize that some students need a tighter rein and that others need more frequent reminders.
- I do my best to keep my own emotions out of the process to give students ample experience with knowing that changing behavior has to do with physical and emotional safety in our learning, not pleasing Andie, the adult.

words." "Solomon, that is yellow behavior. Please move your clip and move to a table to find your best learner self."

I realize I am talking way too much. So I tell them, "I feel frustrated when you keep talking over friends because you're not listening to them. I know you know how to ask questions; you've been asking them this week. But this morning, you're not asking them. Let's look at the class promises."

As we revisit our list of promises, students seem able to focus, and we manage to finish the strategy work. But I notice something when we looked at the class promises. "Being nice" is important, but there is a deeper layer that we haven't identified yet.

The formation of our circle of trust is cyclical. For example, at the beginning of the year, the student-generated class promises focus on being nice to each other, cleaning up our work spaces, and "kissing owies."

This student-created list sends a clear message that our jobs are to work together as best as each five- and six-year-old and forty-one-year-old can, based on our life experiences outside of school. When problems arise in our room, rereading the class promises often helps all of us return to that original "feel safe like at home" intention. But midway through this school year, we realize the promises are not meeting all the needs of our community.

The Circle of Respect

Conflict in February is familiar. In a tide pool, the energy of the water ebbs and flows, much like the energy and engagement of students in our kindergarten tide pool. Different times of the year, different times of the day, and interruptions in usual patterns all affect the organisms in our classroom. By midyear, students are confident about their role in our community, but our learning environment has changed significantly since the beginning of the school year. In the complex ecosystem of the classroom, we enter deeper levels in our literacy conversations.

When we realize the class promises are no longer working for our circle, I decide it is time to have a class meeting. It takes us four meetings to reach a solution.

The students' goals have not changed since we wrote the first set of class promises. Once again, they bring up the need to "be quiet,"

"take turns," "listen to each other," and "look at each other." But they also teach me that there is an element of risk for them I hadn't realized. The children tell me the circle seems like being on stage, and they compare it to an assembly they have recently seen in the school gymnasium. This really surprises me; I have done everything I can to make speaking in the circle comfortable.

But the reality is, it is both exciting and scary to share what you know with an audience. For many students, this is the first time they have spoken formally in front of their peers. To take that risk, each speaker expects to be listened to—and they expect their message to be understood. But that is a difficult expectation for each listener, all the time, in every circle.

The notion of a "circle of respect" emerges from our discussions. Bao Jun alters the course of our conversation with her comment that "You have to respect someone who's talking." Her words trigger a litany of responses:

"You can be kind and listen to their words and give them what they need." (Cole)

"You have to respect people when they are sharing at show-and-tell. When someone is talking, respect them." (Byron)

"Share something that you have." (Leteshia)

"Be quiet when others are talking." (Sabinna)

Respect is at the heart of our discussion. As a class, we speak the promises that are important to us when we meet in the circle. We vote to call our gatherings a "circle of respect." Now, our promises hang on a round poster above our meeting area. These words hover just above us and serve as a gentle reminder of all we intend to do when we listen to each other (see Figure 5.15).

Much like the comprehension strategies, building community is not simply a series of activities. It can be difficult for classroom teachers to make time for something we think we have already addressed. But when we carve out the time to set expectations for our community, we are better able to listen and trust each person, and to learn side by side.

Nests and Communities

In the middle of digging deeper into nests, Sidney lights up with an idea. "Andie! We could make nests!" And with a smile on my face, I confirm the possibility. I know Sidney and I are on the same wavelength—and that by the end of the week, we will make nests.

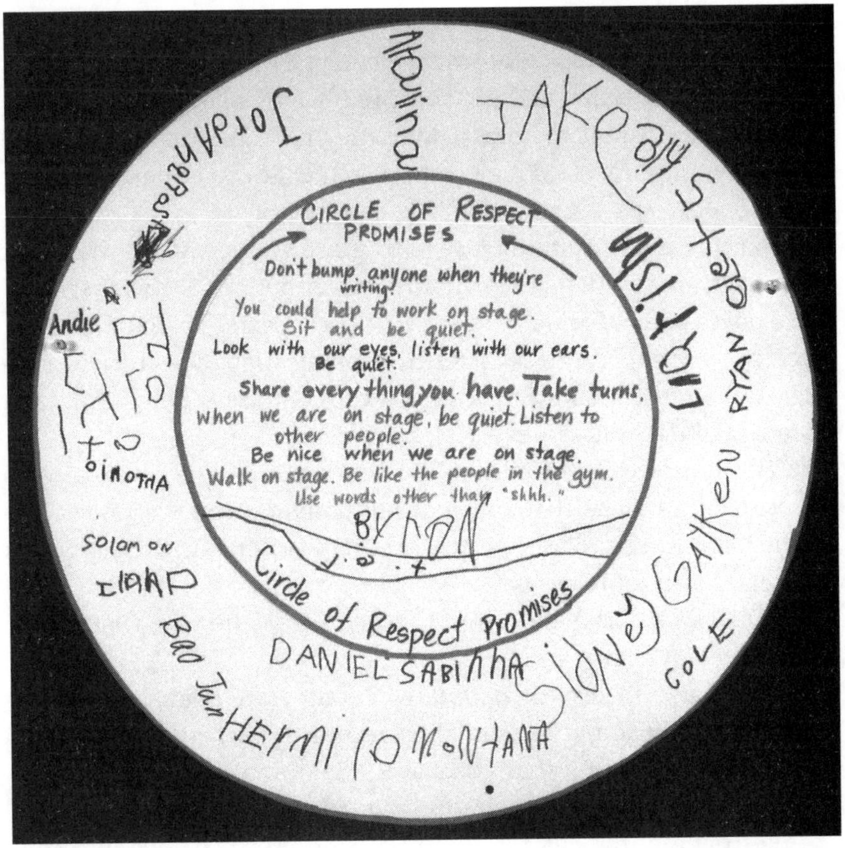

Figure 5.15 The circle of
respect promises.

In preparation, I bring in six genuine birds' nests from a variety of birds. They are made with thorns, twigs, mud, horsehair, and other mystery ingredients. Wearing latex gloves, we examine and touch the nests. We read the book *Birds Build Nests* by Yvonne Winer (2002), a picture book written in poem form showing birds in their natural habitats. Then we search for nest material outside, gathering small sticks, grass, and fir cones. Back in the classroom, we pull out our bags of personal nest material, and I offer yarn and clay as additional nest-building ingredients. (Some of the children even add their own hair!)

"Your job, my winged friends, is to make a nest for your family," I tell the children. As students sit to build their nests, the room grows quiet. I notice they are sitting in different groups than they often choose. Leteshia sits with Antonio and Ryan; Jake is working by himself.

It takes them about twenty minutes to create their nests. Their work is focused and careful. Alma lays grass strand by strand, Ryan layers piece over piece, and Hermilo decides to start over again after getting frustrated with his first attempt. As I eavesdrop on conversations around the room, I realize how far we have come as a community.

Antonio asks Bao Jun, "Do you draw with feathers in China?"

Bao Jun says, "Yeah."

"Do you have clay in China?" Antonio asks.

"I make clay in China!" she tells him.

Antonio sneezes, and Ryan immediately says, "Bless you!"

"Thank you," Antonio says.

"You're welcome."

When Jake completes his nest, he stands and walks over to the next table and asks a question I have never heard him ask: "Do you think it's good?"

Leteshia examines it and pronounces, "It's perfect!" Ryan and Antonio chime in with compliments as well. Was this the same class that needed time and space to write new promises for our work together just weeks ago?

It is now possible for them to share their creations and hear honest and genuine compliments on work created in our community. I notice a sense of trust in their conversations. The compliments continue throughout the morning and even as students gather their nests to take them home. Leteshia is right: Jake's nest—all the nests—are perfect.

Spiraling Deeper: Determining Importance and Inferring

A new poster hangs from the ceiling: "Determining Importance." *"Los ideas especiales que le escondido"* is the translation I choose for my students: "The special ideas that are hidden" (see Figure 6.1). I am framing the reading strategy a little differently than I have in the past. Last year, I used nonfiction

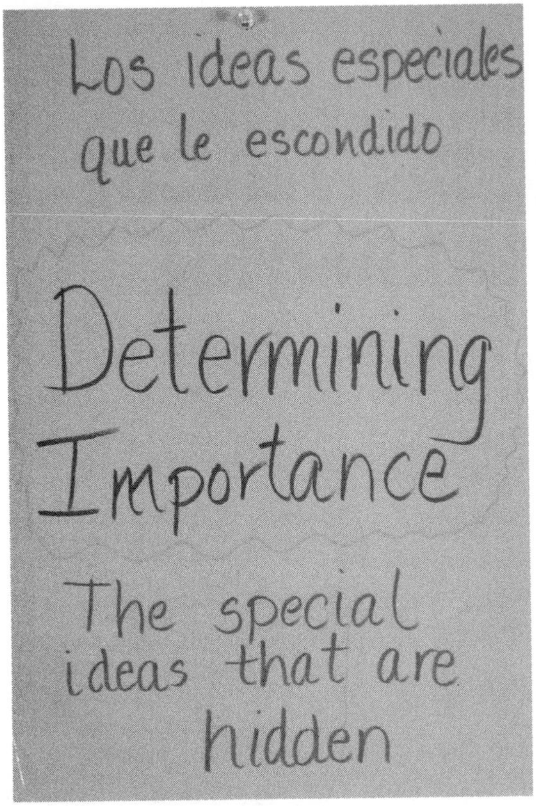

Los ideas especiales
que le escondido

Determining
Importance

The special
ideas that are
hidden

Figure 6.1 Determining Importance poster.

books to bolster their knowledge of animals as we explored finding new information and determining importance.

This year, we've worked with a lot of nonfiction with our close look at owls and birds and the animal home studies. As our community of readers grapples with new strategies, I am drawn to fictional texts with complex ideas. For these students, for this year, I decide on *The Growing-up Tree* to begin our study of what Ellin Keene calls determining "the essence of texts" (Keene and Zimmermann 1997). *The Growing-up Tree* (Rosenberry 2003) tells the story of a boy, his mother, and an apple tree. The mother plants an apple seed when the boy is a baby, and readers follow two life spans: boy to man to grandfather, and seedling to mature apple tree. It is also a perfect book for the spring season, with the timely themes of abundance and growth (see Chapter 4).

On Monday morning, I show the students the cover of *The Growing-up Tree* and ask them to make a prediction about what happens in the book. Alma thinks it's about "the tree . . . it was growing and growing and the kid was trying to get an apple."

Sabinna thinks, "He's trying to get all of the apples off of the tree for his family to eat."

I point to the "Determining Importance" poster and tell them we are going to start working on a new strategy. When I planned how to introduce the strategy, I decided we ought to start with a learning tool with which we are already familiar: webs. I read the book aloud, modeling what's important to me as a reader. I track my thinking on a web I create on the class chart. My mini-lesson is brief, but sets the stage for the students' extended work the next day.

On the second day of our study, we gather in our circle for reading workshop and I hold up the book. "I'm going to read the book again," I tell the children. "Store in your brain everything you think

is important as I read." The room is quiet and I notice their concentration as I read.

When I close the book, I give each student a large piece of paper (12½-by-24-inches) with "The Growing-up Tree" written in the middle.

First, I ask them to draw a tree next to the words, and to draw a circle around the words and the tree. I want them to know what the words say and remember that their ideas connect to the book itself. "Now," I tell them, "your job is to create your own web with what is important to you in the book."

Webs are a good choice to help Byron learn the new strategy. He is comfortable with webs and communicates what's important in the book through the pieces he includes on his web (see Figure 6.2). His web shows me his growing willingness to take risks in his literacy communication. Some ideas are still in pictures, such as the lightning bolt, and others are written with letters representing the sounds he hears. For example, the important information that Alfred died is all communicated through the letters: AfrD IDM. Our work in writing workshop is spilling over into his writing during reading, and I celebrate that he is initiating writing his own messages.

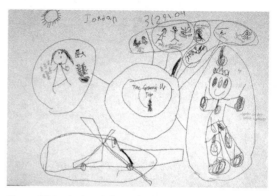

Figure 6.2 Byron's web from *The Growing-up Tree.*

Figure 6.3 Jordan's web from *The Growing-up Tree.*

When I first look at Jordan's web, I am confused. She has drawn a car and a large person with apples on his shirt and pants.

"Jordan, help me understand what the car and the clothes have to do with the book."

After a lengthy pause, she admits, "The car has nothing to do with the book, Andie." As we work together, I am able to redirect her tangent back to a web that works for her. I ask Jordan what is important to her about the book, and after I hear her share several situations from it, I leave her to finish her web. Her completed product shows a more accurate representation of what is important to her in the story. She draws pictures of the woman planting the tree, rocking the baby, and "Mom eating an apple" (see Figure 6.3).

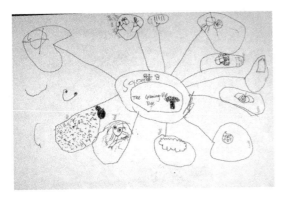

Figure 6.4 Solomon's web from *The Growing-up Tree.*

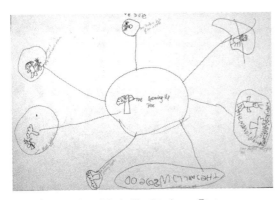

Figure 6.5 Jesse's web from *The Growing-up Tree.*

Jordan's web shows she has found her "essence" of the text: the "growing-up" part of the life cycle.

Solomon's "essence" is focused around the seed, apples, and tree as well. But he adds a new theme from the story that is critical for him. His web includes a picture of rain and wind and clouds, all from the stormy night when both the tree and the man die (see Figure 6.4).

Like Solomon, Jesse articulates the full life cycle through death. Jesse is more comfortable with the written word, and his web reflects that comfort. Though he includes pictures, the power is in his writing: "The man dided happy; the tree dided happy." He remembers the words from the story, "The apple was so good," and writes them in his own invented spelling (see Figure 6.5).

I use the webs the next week as a lens to measure students' growth in a much more difficult text. *The Roses in My Carpet* (Khan 1998) details the struggle of a young Afghani boy living in a refugee camp. He finds an escape from the terror-filled planes and bombs as he weaves colorful carpets. As I look at the student-created webs from this story, I notice fewer drawings and less information about what might have been important about the book to each reader. Jordan has drawn a car again, but this time, her solitary picture represents a key incident in the book: when the boy's sister is struck by a car.

Byron's three pictures are small and carefully drawn. In two of them, he uses writing to label his drawings: FAR for flower and KRPT for carpet.

Solomon includes details that seemed to be lost on other readers, such as darkness, and the mud at the boy's camp. He tells me when he completes his web, "There's no more room for the kid."

Jesse's sparse web shows four pictures that are stick-figure symbols of what's important to him in the story. In all four of these spaces, he uses words to label his drawn figures.

The students are confident using webs as a tool; they show what is important to them in the story. My instincts told me this would be a difficult story to use in a kindergarten classroom. The students' work confirms for me that although their webs are adequate, they may be unfamiliar with the deeper life experiences that I think are the essence of the text. The students are clearly challenged by the text, but they are engaged with it, they learn from it, and they are able to communicate what makes sense to them.

Determining importance lends itself to integration with other classroom studies. For example, for the study of courage, we investigated what is important for courage: Who is courageous? How do we know? How are animals courageous and how do they show it? How do we show our courage? Ultimately, the children had the choice to draw, paint, dance, sing, write, or move to represent courage.

The strategy of determining importance was used to frame our expert focus on tunnels, playhouses, tree houses, clubhouses, and houses of art. We read books to expand our knowledge of tunnels, documenting "obvious clues" and "hidden clues" in our research. With the book *Once There Was a Tree* (Romanova 1989) we explored how animals make and live in tunnels, and we talked about living in trees. This picture book details what beings—human and animal—use tree stumps and invites the reader to explore the question, who owns trees in a forest?

Determining importance flows naturally into drawing inferences, allowing us to create emotional intimacy with the texts we are studying. The students made a strong connection to the book *Once There Was a Tree*. They loved it so much that I decided to use the book again to frame our beginning steps in a new strategy: inferences. As we read the book several times that week, students appeared to be thankful to return to it again and again.

"It's Like Making a New Book": Inferences

Inferences are vital in comprehending what we read. Proficient readers make simple and complex inferences, often without even being aware of it. In *Mosaic of Thought* (1997), Ellin Keene and Susan Zimmermann write:

To infer as we read is to go beyond literal interpretation and to open a world of meaning deeply connected to our lives. We create an original meaning, a meaning born at the intersection of our background knowledge (schema), the words printed on a page, and our mind's capacity to merge that combination into something uniquely ours. We go beyond the literal and weave our own sense into the words we read. As we read further, that meaning is revised, enriched, sometimes abandoned, based on what we continue to read. (p. 149)

Dylan's mom gives us a tremendous gift when she volunteers to make a new inference poster for the class. Her finished product intrigues the students, inviting them to explore inferring. On the poster, she has glued three-dimensional objects to illustrate the words "schema plus book clues equals bridges to new knowing" (see Figure 6.6). When explaining what an inference is, I always talk about how schema and the clues from the book help the reader connect to new knowing, but I had not found a way to *show* them.

When the students see the poster she made, they rise to the difficult challenge of the concept because they recognize all the pieces. They are familiar with the ideas the poster represents, and

Figure 6.6 Inferring poster.

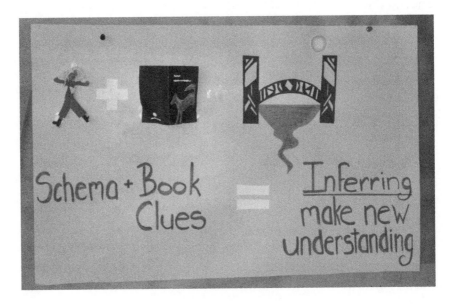

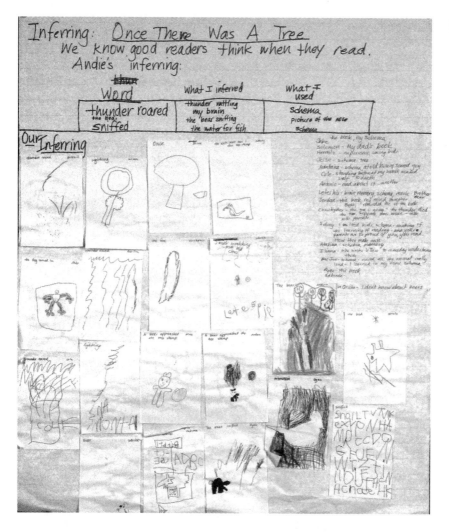

Figure 6.7 Inferring: *Once There Was a Tree.*

they bring a confidence for using a new comprehension strategy that builds on what they know.

When I model inferring with the book *Once There Was a Tree* in our first reading workshop of the week, I introduce the strategy with the poster and tell the children what phrases in the book stump me. For example, I choose the words "thunder roared" to infer publicly with the class. I write the words on our three-column anchor chart (Miller 2002) (see Figure 6.7). I look up with the book close to my chest, signaling to the children that I am about to make a significant explanation. Aloud, I relive the story of thunder booming off the thirteen-thousand-foot peaks that surround me

on a Colorado hiking trip. The thunder that day rattled my brain and body. I jot down the inference I make from the book and my experience and show them how my experience helped me understand the author's words, "thunder roared." Finally, I share with the students what thinking I used to create my new understanding. Even though the book has nothing to do with mountains or climbing, I used my schema and the words in the book to "go beyond a literal interpretation" and realize that thunder rattles forests like it rattled me.

The next day, we return to the chart so the students can add their own inferences. On sticky notes, Leteshia and Jordan write of the movie *Brother Bear,* a children's film they have seen in the theater, and they make connections between the book and the movie. I want them to verbalize how they used their brains to make connections, so now our chart includes three columns: the word or phrase that stumped us; what we inferred; and what part of our brains we used (Miller 2002). I open the conversation to include all of us; the children need to hear what others around them have used from their life experiences to make sense of the book.

Iliana, a native Spanish speaker who rarely speaks in either language, is stumped by the word "sniffed." She fills a sticky note with letters. When I ask her what she understands about "sniffed," she tells me she writes letters to someday understand them. These three examples from Leteshia, Jordan, and Iliana show that although we are on the right track, the students are not yet making the bridges I believe they can make.

A Story for Bear

The next week, we practice inferring with a new book. At Antonio's request, I read *A Story for Bear* (Haseley 2002) all the way through, "with no stopping." As a teacher, I have a hard time not modeling my thinking as I read. But I know it is important to honor his request to hear the whole story without interrupting *his* thinking. Our new anchor chart holds my two "post-reading" attempts at inferring (see Figure 6.8).

The top of the chart reads, "We know great readers infer to make new understandings." *A Story for Bear* offers us a multitude of pathways for new and potentially deeper understandings. This book tells the story of the growing friendship between a wild bear and a woman who is living in the forest for the summer. Their

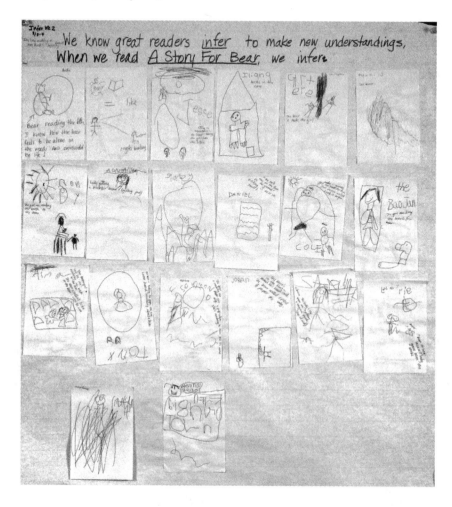

Figure 6.8 Inferring: *A Story for Bear.*

friendship is based on the books she reads to the bear and his emotions as she reads aloud to him. Although the book is text heavy, I see students willing to muddle through the many words, sustaining their interest in this magical tale.

Daniel confirms for me his willingness to dig into a difficult strategy when he compares inferences to "making a new book." His smile says, "Andie, I get it."

The children's sticky notes on our anchor chart prove to me that they, too, are truly able to make inferences as they grapple with this difficult text. Jesse's picture shows the bear sitting on the mountain (see Figure 6.9). I have to be patient and ask him what he means by this. It takes time for me to understand what the students are inferring—and it takes Jesse time to describe it. He tells

Figure 6.9 Jesse's inference sticky note.

Figure 6.10 Daniel's inference sticky note.

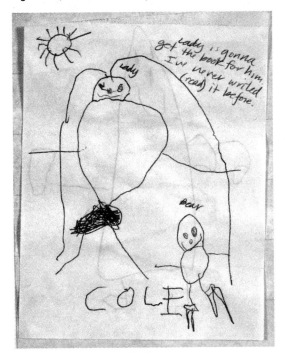

Figure 6.11 Cole's inference sticky note.

me, "He keeps hearing the girl from the letter." Here, Jesse infers about the voice that the bear hears when he looks at a letter he finds.

Daniel writes about the letter as well. He has drawn a large picture of a written letter. One solitary tree implies the setting of the story (see Figure 6.10). Daniel tells me, "The note was on the floor on the ground. Writing is new in the forest."

Cole focuses on a different key point, one that is central for him. He draws a picture of the woman and the bear and tells me, "The lady is gonna get the book for him. I've never writed it before" (see Figure 6.11). When I ask him what he means by "writed," he tells me he means that he read it.

Inferences and Tea Parties

The children love our tea parties. As a teacher, I notice that the tea parties often help me identify what the next step should be. But besides the educational value, the students derive such great joy from the tea parties that we return to them a couple of times a month.

Tea parties seem like the ideal way to invite conversations in a small group. This time, because we are so familiar with our teas, we decide to expand the size of each party. We start by dividing into two large groups, and Ruth and I ask our groups the same two questions to frame our conversations: "What gift of the heart did the woman give the bear?" and "What gift of the heart did the bear give the woman?" By asking the children these two questions, I hope to focus their mental lenses on the relationships within the book. These questions can be answered only by making inferences about the characters and the ways they interact.

Bao Jun starts off the conversation at one tea party with the words, "The girl give the bear a part of her heart."

Sidney makes a compelling inference when she says that there is a gift the bear wishes he could give: "The bear wishes he could read to her."

The conversations are rich, and I am pleased with how students build their comments on what other students say. For the tea party dialogues to work, I need to unpack what the children say, and not just the first time they say it. Solomon, for example, frames his inferences at two different times in our conversation. He opens one of the discussion groups by attempting to explain what he knows. "The bear was taking a book to river. The bear gave to girl."

Jesse builds on this comment by saying, "The girl gave it to the bear, because on the page [you can see] where she left the carpet of books."

Other students contribute to the conversation, then Solomon shares again, saying, "They both give each other. You get some book, your favorite book to read [pause] the woman."

As a teacher, I know I can attempt to make sense of his two inferences separately, or I can go beyond my initial assumptions and see what Solomon intends for us to know. At first, it appears that Solomon is mistaken, talking about the bear giving a book to

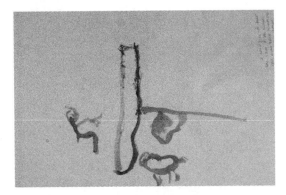

Figure 6.12 Daniel's inference painting.

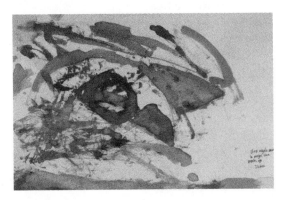

Figure 6.13 Iliana's inference painting.

the girl. But Solomon fleshes out more details in his second statement. He realizes they gave to each other, even if it wasn't a tangible object: they gave each other the gift of friendship. It takes Solomon some time and listening to classmates to be able to explain what he is learning about the relationship between the woman and the bear.

Solomon has a keen mind and the intention to make sense of the book. Despite his good playground English, his native Hmong is not spoken at school, and I know he sometimes struggles to communicate. Solomon teaches me that I need to wait for students to explain what they know, and I need to give them time to process their comprehension.

After our tea and chocolate chip cookies, I gather the children together to give the following instructions: "Friends, your job is to paint a picture of a gift from your heart that you would give to the woman or the bear."

Daniel's painting is framed by his words, "I would give the bear the same thing the woman did: listen, 'cause he was shy" (see Figure 6.12). Daniel can read chapter books at the first-grade level, but he doesn't often make significant responses to our classroom work. I wonder what allows him to make such a significant inference this time. It might be the book itself, the painting, the time, or the conversation. It almost doesn't matter—what's important is the reminder to me that he is capable of such a hidden connection.

Iliana, who is usually silent, helps us understand her better in our project. She tells me, *"Una regalo para la mujer. Una papeles hoja"* (see Figure 6.13). Loosely translated, I interpret her words to mean she would give the woman leaves of paper for a gift. When Iliana offers us the gifts of her words, we listen and learn about a girl whose language often isolates her. We also find how she is making sense in our predominantly English read-alouds and classroom conversations.

Sabinna—with her eyes on communication—decides her present would be writing and drawing tools for the woman. Her painting is abstract, but her gift ideas are clear to her audience (see Figure 6.14).

Weslandia: *Moving into New Worlds*

Figure 6.14 Sabinna's inference painting.

We launch into our final week of focused study of inferences with a favorite book of mine, *Weslandia* (Fleischman 2000). A boy has his backyard planted with mysterious seeds and creates a new civilization in his quest to build a meaningful summer project. He is transformed from neighborhood scapegoat to revered king of his territory.

It is May, and I am willing to risk reading a multileveled book to my students. It is not new to them now to make inferences. I read the book aloud and share with them my inferences on a large class chart. I know some parts are confusing to them, and I want to identify those parts. It's time for them to rely less on me and more on their classmates as they work through their confusion. At this time of the year, I think they are ready for more independent group work, and I structure our learning prompts through the week with that in mind.

"We are going to take another look at *Weslandia*. We've read this book twice, and I am wondering what parts still confuse you. What I was thinking we'd do is take a picture walk. I have small sticky notes, and when we reach a page that confuses you, wiggle your hand. I will put a sticky note on the page to remind us later. I am not going to read the words. Wiggle your fingers a lot if you feel confused."

With fingers wiggling, the children share their confusion. Sidney opens a new door for us when she says, "This page makes me feel kind of weird."

I ask her if she feels it inside her body. She nods and explains that she feels weird in her tummy. Bao Jun tells us, "I feel it in my heart." And Jesse adds, "When I don't get it, I feel it in my brain."

I appreciate this chance for us to talk about that "gut feeling"—how intuition can lead you to identify your confusion.

After putting sticky notes on the four pages that seem most confusing to the children, we act out what we don't understand in small groups. I tell the children, "If you are most confused by this page, stand up." I send that group of students to a section of the room to figure out how to act like that page. I continue through the four pages, being sure every student finds a confusing section to move like. "You have thirty seconds to figure out how to act like what's happening on the page. When you come back, you'll do that movement in front of the whole group to make an inference."

When they return to the circle, I ask, "How did you take your schema and the book clues and make new knowing?" My question is meant as a starting point for us to explore our confusion together. Byron, always willing to share with anyone who will listen, starts off our hard work. He shapes his body into one of the wooden chairs of the book, and then recognizes that the boy in the book "made the wood chair."

Alma notices that Jake and his friends are "playing the game like in the book."

Sabinna has a different interpretation of the game that is played in the book. She tells us it's "like how they fighted in the game."

It really helps them to act out in groups the pages that were confusing. They need to have discussions together without me there to make sense of things. They need the space to talk—and also to move—-to connect to their new knowing.

We've traveled in a dramatic and dedicated direction all year. Distant in my memory is the first book I read aloud to a group of five-year-olds who could hardly sit still for fifteen pages of short text. I remember Allison's first invitation, the opening that escorted us into exploring metacognition and schema. I can see Byron excitedly drawing his mental images of sleeping in blankets of snow from *Imagine a Night* (Gonsalves 2003). I hear Daniel's voice connecting his schema to the story and creating a new book in his mind, through words and actions.

The strategies keep us spiraling deeper, creating a community of knowing together. As the end of the school year beckons and I realize my time with these children is coming to a close, I look forward to learning more about them through our last strategy, synthesis.

Standing in the Waves: Synthesizing Information

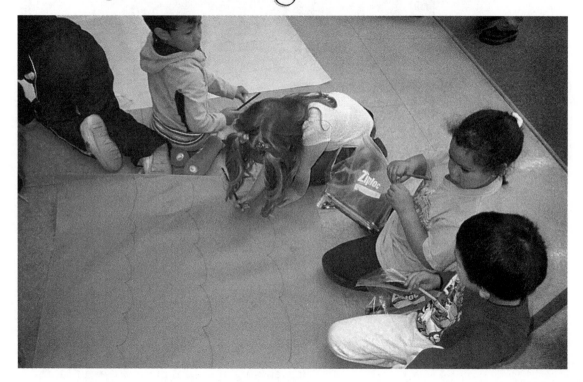

It's Thursday morning and the clean-up music plays, calling the students to pick up books, math manipulatives, and building materials and head to the morning circle. Cole is back at school after being sick, and his eyes light on our new synthesis poster. In the poster, two arms hold binoculars with the words "The Book" on the lenses. Behind the binoculars, a representation of the world fills the page (see Figure 7.1).

"Andie, what's this?" he asks me with a smile.

"What a great question!" I turn to the class, and ask, "Friends, did you hear Cole's question? Can you tell him what the poster means?"

Figure 7.1 Synthesis poster.

"It's synthesis," Jake tells Cole.

"Can you explain synthesis to him?" I prod.

Daniel takes a deep breath and goes for it: "It means schema and book clues and new understanding all put together. It's like inferring but . . . more."

Leteshia nods. "It's learning and thinking inside your brain."

Sidney agrees, but makes a revision. "It's about the learning *of* the thinking of your brain."

"And you need book clues," Jake adds.

Solomon points to the waves and bull's-eye drawings on either side of the poster: "You pick which one to draw, waves or a circle."

"Thanks for explaining to Cole with such clear words. This is a brand new poster, Cole. Let's read it together."

We all recite in English and then Spanish: "Synthesis. The beautiful way you live through the book. *El viaje bonita que se vive en el libro.*"

Kindergartners and Synthesis

When teachers talk about the strategy of synthesis, kindergartners synthesizing information is not usually part of the discussion. Teachers tend to think the most important literacy focus for five- and six-year-olds centers on surface structure. I remember conversations with colleagues worried about end-of-the-year assessments and young learners in phonemic awareness activities: "What letters and sounds do my kindergartners know?" That's certainly part of what I think about, but since working with the comprehension strategies, I'm focusing more on what Ellin Keene and Susan Zimmerman call "deep structure" (1997).

I'm more and more convinced of the age appropriateness and even necessity of deep structure study for kindergarten students. But synthesis? Will they be able to use this strategy to make sense of books and to communicate that understanding?

What Is Synthesis?

I agree with Stephanie Harvey that synthesis is the most complex of the comprehension strategies (Harvey and Goudvis 2000). She writes:

> A true synthesis is an Aha! of sorts. . . . Synthesizing lies on a continuum of evolving thinking. Synthesizing runs the gamut from taking stock of meaning while reading to achieving new insight. . . . A true synthesis is achieved when a new perspective or thought is born out of the reading. (p. 144)

When I was teaching a graduate course titled Reading Workshop a couple of years ago, I went through each of the comprehension strategies, practicing and identifying how we use them as knowledgeable readers. I found that synthesis was the most difficult strategy for me and my adult learners to attend to in difficult texts. Synthesis is many things. Yes, it's retellings, and yes, it's making personal connections to the text, and yes, it's discovering new aha's. But synthesis is more than a list of ways to interact with the text; it transcends the text.

I believe synthesis has the potential to be not only the most fluid retelling tool I use, but also a door to walk through together

as the students and I create a new environment of understanding. Originally, when I contemplated which strategies to teach the kindergartners, I wondered what would happen if we grappled with synthesis together.

Teaching Synthesis

We enter into the world of synthesis late in the school year. While we have worked with the other comprehension strategies, we have also honed our skills for reading aloud together. The students are showing a deeper respect when someone gets in their way of seeing the book ("Anthony, I can't see. Can you please sit down?") instead of crying out, grabbing the person in the way, or talking to someone next to them. They allow themselves to join me in the mystery of the book. They set themselves up for knowing the book for the first time as well as for digging into it with me and the others in our room. I have learned how to authentically invite them, and I allow myself to enter the new world of knowing with them.

Earlier one year, the students had chosen four major topics for us to study, and one was butterflies. During May and June, we studied animals, ourselves, and courage, and we watched live caterpillars grow into painted-lady butterflies until we released them in June. In *Reading with Meaning,* Debbie Miller (2002) explains how she uses circles to diagram thinking in synthesis, and I use her circle idea while unpacking my own synthesis after my first read-aloud of *The Prince of Butterflies* (Coville 2002). I think about what my students would need. I remember how hard it is for Spencer to draw, especially something like ripples in a pond. This leads me to structuring my first mini-lesson a little differently.

I begin by introducing the students to the potential motion of synthesis. I lead this first lesson, reading the book through for the first time, noting aloud what changes my thinking. Next, I decide to model two picture metaphors to document our changing thinking. Using both the metaphor that Miller uses—the ripples in the pond—and a new metaphor, a tide pool with waves, the children and I wander into synthesis slowly and deliberately (see Figure 7.2).

When I am ready to invite the students to draw and detail *their* synthesis, I reread the book and ask them to choose which picture metaphor fits them better, the circle idea or waves.

Figure 7.2 Andie shows her synthesis chart.

I remind them of how I showed my changing thinking yesterday. "So, you can do your thinking with rings, like I did, or I have another idea: waves. When I think of waves, I draw them like this, with peaks. It looks like water; it looks like waves." I draw four lines of waves across the butcher paper. "Where would you draw your first picture?"

The students and I work through where we place our changing thinking on each type of recording paper. I want to be sure that they know how to order their thinking on the written page—and I want to be sure they are documenting their own changes in thought, not mine. Then, I send them off to have their first try at documenting their synthesis.

Students' First Synthesis Drawings

In *The Prince of Butterflies,* we meet a person who devotes his life to saving butterflies. When he is young, butterflies speak to him and ask him for help. For several years as an adolescent, the boy transforms into a butterfly and guides the whole community of butterflies to the next resting place on their migratory path. At the end of the book, the butterflies return to the now eighty-year-old man to support him at this stage of his life.

Figure 7.3 Dylan's synthesis.

Figure 7.4 Tyler's synthesis.

When I look at the students' work in response to *The Prince of Butterflies* from that first day, I see proof that five- and six-year-olds can synthesize difficult text. For example, in Dylan's first thinking, he shows the boy standing frozen as he stares at the butterflies. Next, he writes the words "Da Mom"—his notations for the words dad and mom—and draws the boy moving away from the house with an arrow. Then he draws the butterflies flying to the boy. In his next wave, he draws the boy's wings as he becomes a butterfly. And finally, he shows the boy flying in the air and returning to the ground (see Figure 7.3). Dylan demonstrates that he understands at least the first two-thirds of the book, using the building blocks of the story to aid in his retelling.

Tyler also uses the chronology of the story in his retelling/synthesis drawing. His picture metaphor is the ripples in the pond rather than the wave metaphor that Dylan uses. The points he chooses are also different (see Figure 7.4). He starts with a butterfly at the center of the circles, and then uses lines to define the butterflies flying onto the boy. In the next ripple, we see the boy metamorphosing into the butterfly. Finally, Tyler draws the boy as an old man in his wheelchair seeing the butterflies come to him once again. Like Dylan, Tyler is able to use the structure to demonstrate his synthesis of the story.

Dylan and Tyler are successful at synthesis when we define synthesis only through a retelling lens. However, Destiny synthesizes the book beyond the chronology of the story. Although her drawing leaves me confused, her explanation of her thinking shows me that she has a deep understanding of the story.

"This boy, he passed the butterflies. He never hurt them, but the butterflies hurt him by never coming back to him. And then the butterflies came back and he was happy again. And he loved the butterflies once again." She paused and added, "At the end, I thought he dies. And the butterflies were really sad inside like him."

I asked how her thinking changed as she heard the story, and again she thought a moment, then responded, "The patches that made me really interested in the story.

Figure 7.5 Spencer's synthesis.

. . . Well, when he smiled at the butterflies and said he'd help them."

Noticing different ways that students are using synthesis to comprehend the text, I worry about Spencer getting frustrated or feeling limited by the drawing structures. A first look at Spencer's drawing might confirm that worry. But when I allow Spencer to help me synthesize *his* work, my new understanding emerges (see Figure 7.5). It's easy to look at his drawing and see a mess. In reality, it is a detailed and intentional map of Spencer's understanding of the story. He is eager to share his thinking, and explains, "It's a map. It's of the guy and these are the butterflies, and he's turning into a butterfly, and then he's going over here, and then he goes over here, and that's his home, and he goes over here, and over here that's the way he goes here. Then here, then here, and over here."

When I try to probe what went on in his head as he heard the story and made the map, he answers with his stock reply, "I don't know. It just did it."

Whereas Destiny is able to use words to explain her thinking, Spencer relies more on his drawing. He, too, can use synthesis as a tool.

The longer I work with these strategies as a teacher, the more I notice how they can aid readers in deepening their levels of understanding. I originally thought synthesis was a retelling tool where the readers added details from their own lives. Work such as Destiny's and Spencer's guided me to change my thinking significantly. I see them "owning" the books they read. I notice they stand in as characters in the book—virtually living through the

book as they think about their own thinking. I notice that my students stand side by side with characters from the books, and that they can talk about their own thinking while thinking for the character as well. They are able to hold the thinking of two beings at once.

Moving to Synthesis

Where Is Grandpa? (Barron and Soentpiet 2001) is a book that has the depth to be explored through synthesis. It is the compassionate story of a young boy's grief when his grandfather dies. His whole family talks about their memories of Grandpa. Adventures in nature, jokes shared, and conversations with him frame the grief process for the family. However, the narrator cannot verbalize the boy's memories until his father answers such questions as, "Where is Grandpa now?"

Knowing that this year's group of students is showing a solid connection to the way movement can help them understand texts, I choose movement as a way to continue our exploration of synthesis.

We are in our second week of synthesis and it's one of those four-day weeks at the end of the school year. I decide to use this precious time to model my own synthesis and invite their demonstrations all on the same day.

"What I'm going to ask you to do today is read along with me as I read *Where Is Grandpa?* I'm going to synthesize and move a little, and then you will."

After reading the book aloud, I physically synthesize in front of the class. I have never tried this before, and I'm not sure it will work. Important parts of the book to which I move include shock at the grandfather's death, being the waterfall, and looking from the tree house to the mountains. At the end, I start to notice I could be in the tree house, see the mountainous landscape, and touch the image of my grandfather. I purposefully smile to show my changed energy around the death of the grandfather: my synthesis.

Returning to my seat, I pick up the book and tell the children it's their turn. "Go live like this book," I tell them. "The whole thing. Act it out."

Around me, children shape their bodies into waterfalls, trees, snowmen, raccoons, and pumpkins, all visually obvious from the

Figure 7.6 Children synthesize through movement by being waterfalls.

illustrations in the text (see Figure 7.6). This is a start for their synthesis. I can't take their body movements at face value. I decide they probably need to share more information so we can know who is synthesizing what.

"Who's ready to show the beautiful way you live through the book?"

I need Alma and Iliana to tell us that they are acting out the sunset that occurs more than once in the book. It's easy for me to imagine they are metaphorically connecting the setting sun with a man dying. But I'm not sure.

Antonio goes through a series of motions, showing us his version of the family's memories. He tells us, "I acted all of them."

"Yes, that's synthesis," I tell him. He understands that his synthesis includes all of the pieces of the story. I wonder if he understands that synthesis is more than retelling the story.

Figure 7.7 Solomon synthesizes "It's a pumpkin" through movement with his friends.

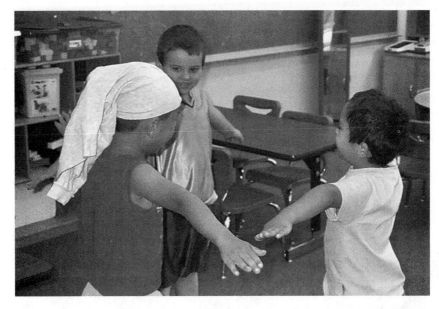

Montana digests the story in a significantly deeper way when he tells us, "The kid waited for his grandpa and he was remembering."

Knowing that it takes several attempts for students to synthesize difficult text, we revisit *Where Is Grandpa?* and our movements. This time, after our second read-aloud, I invite them to "go live through this book in your life."

Solomon pulls the neck of his long-sleeved T-shirt over his hair (see Figure 7.7). His invention confuses me until I ask him what his shirt is for. He says, "It's a pumpkin, Andie! I'm the grandpa scaring the mom."

Raccoons fill our room as many students act like the furry creatures which play a role in one of the memories the father recalls about his childhood. Some students, like Byron, enact the page from the book where the raccoons are in the top of a tree (see Figure 7.8). But Atalina crawls on the floor to show the raccoons looking for food, an idea that is not in the book.

I am grateful for Atalina's inference because this gives me a chance to steer the conversation to a discussion of inferences. Though you don't have to infer to synthesize, I notice it helps the students—Atalina in particular—to move beyond a simple retelling. Bao Jun, Jake, and Christopher also share their inferences.

Figure 7.8 Byron being a racoon in a tree.

To close our synthesis on *Where Is Grandpa?*, I ask the students, "What's the big idea in this book? *Que es la idea grande?* What do you think the author wanted us to learn?"

Cole's wisdom about the book is evident in his answer: "I'm thinking the kid wanted you to know about Grandpa. And he wanted you to learn about heaven."

Sidney nods and adds, "Yeah, the author really wants us to learn about what happened to Grandpa and where he went."

I avoid initiating discussions about faith. But my students don't. In fact, death and heaven are always linked in the worlds of my five- and six-year-olds. We can't talk about death without several of my students bringing in the word "heaven." No matter what their faith, it is in their schema and it affects the conversations in our room.

Once again, the comprehension strategies have offered us a platform for discussion that we never would have had otherwise. Our synthesis runs the gamut from exploring what it feels like to have a pumpkin on your head and seeing raccoons in a tree to realizing what it's like to be a sunset and to have your grandfather die. Cole knows that the book is more than a catalog of events in the grandfather's life. In working with his own synthesis, Cole finds his way to live life through the eyes of the boy.

Synthesizing Kindergarten

The comprehension strategies offer us a framework to start from and return to as our learning grows, as we live side by side in the classroom. Our class promises and circle of respect promises act as community strategies, touchstones we start from and return to as we build trust together.

As I look back over these past two years, I realize that I have relied on the comprehension strategies to deepen my understanding as I "read" the text that is my classroom. How has my thinking evolved? What "aha's" have I experienced on the road to new insights? What have the children taught me?

A crucial change I went through as a teacher is learning how to let myself be a friend to my students, and in turn, letting them be friends to me. This relationship is founded on trust. Trust plays an enormous role in learning, even though we teachers seldom if ever talk about it.

Trust requires more than simple acceptance of each other. I knew that my students were starting to trust me when Allison was able to tell me she didn't understand what we were reading in October. My excitement at that moment was as much for Allison initiating our comprehension strategy study as it was for the growth of trust in our community.

Using authentic, high-quality literature that offers unique and realistic connections for each learner in our room extends our work beyond creating a simple community. It allows us to use books to talk about death and heaven, prison and loss. Great literature offers older readers those kinds of opportunities; young learners deserve to experience and grow through literature as well. We bring our life stories and experiences to the books we read and to the friends who sit beside us.

These kindergartners have taught me that they learn like I do. We all want to take time to explore what we are passionate about, and share our excitement with people we trust. We want our fears to be as welcome as our playfulness, and our silences to be as accepted as our words. We want to take risks big and small in an environment that nurtures us, and at the same time nudges us to learn in this kindergarten tide pool we have created together.

Acknowledgments

Namaste: I honor the place in you in which the entire universe dwells. I honor the place in you in which is love, of truth, of light and of peace. When you are in that place in you, and I am in that place in me, we are one.

We are most indebted to the geniuses who graced Andie's classroom for the past two years. Their generous teaching, their consistent ability to forgive, and the way they lived the touchstones all served as inspiration for both of us. We thank their parents for enjoying and learning from our class of friends. *Namaste.*

Barbara Hicks, the principal at Harold Oliver Primary has supported Andie's teaching by listening, visiting, and offering insights, all with gentleness and trust. She welcomed Ruth wholeheartedly into the school community, making time to talk in the midst of her busy school day. *Namaste.*

Peggy Albertine, Jeanne Robin, and Sarah Taylor are the kindergarten teacher educators at Harold Oliver Primary who consistently inquired about this book. Though they avoided the tape recording devises planted in the room, we hear their voices as colleagues in learning. *Namaste.*

Brenda Power must serve as the Queen of all editors. She believed in this project from the start and she shepherded us through the process from proposal to finished product. Through gifts, notes, and classroom visits, Brenda's incredible spirit of encouragement invigorated us. We are grateful for her talent at reading our work and helping us craft our message. We know she spent more hours than we can imagine helping us reorganize, shape, and revise the book. Her vision helped us imagine our audience, and gave us the direction we needed. *Namaste*.

We love our Courage to Teach community. We know we are better teachers and listeners because of the wise facilitators we stand beside as well as our local Courage groups. They are an ever-present Circle of Trust for us. We particularly thank Virginia Shorey, Caryl Casbon, Greg Smith, Matt Lyon, Marcy Jackson, and Rick Jackson. *Namaste* to all.

Though we have been one in the writing of this book, we wish to extend our individual thanks.

I send a world of thanks to my family who are spread across the United States. Mary and David both wondered what their sister was attempting. They and my Dad supported me amidst my confusion and celebration. I can hear their laughter from here. Mom, I think you gave me the writing gene. Thanks for reading drafts and offering encouragement from the very beginning.

Jim, thank you for all of those hours you spent—with Ruth and without—taking stills, perfecting photographs, and creating CDs for this book. You make the difficult world of computers look easy.

Ruth, your wisdom first guided me years ago in your Language Acquisition class. With that crafty grin on your face, you invited me to look deeply into the lives of my students, and you gently encouraged me to peer into the world of my own inner teacher. For all of the moments we have shared in my classroom, in the Courage to Teach work, at Lewis & Clark College, and with our families together, for all the words written and shared, both here on these pages and in our own silences, I am deeply grateful.

The experience of writing this book with you has proved to me what amazing gifts and miraculous messages true community offers: communal knowing.

Laurie and Alysa, thank you for patiently witnessing the writing of this book. Alysa, you served brilliantly as kindergarten test

monkey while also being daughter incredible in moments beyond counting. Will you please keep coming to my class and continue to help me see my friends more clearly? Laurie, my soul's mate, throughout this project your support and words and actions amazed and encouraged me, buoyed and supported me, in the moments where I was sure of my truths and in the minutes when I wasn't. I appreciate your quiet encouragement and joy as I continue to plant myself in environments that I deeply love. Thank you for walking this life journey with me, side by side, helping me see what is truly most important: living each moment in the light of love.

    Namaste,
Andie

Andie, I am grateful beyond words for all you have taught me. (But I'll try anyway!) You ask me the tough questions and work with me to answer them. I appreciate your way with words, courage with ideas, and compassion for all your students. Thanks for your weekly memos, poems about the classroom, and willingness to craft our prose together. I look forward to our writing and teaching partnership continuing to grow. I thank you and Laurie for sharing your time with Alysa. She brings me back into the world of childhood through her joy in our tea parties, in art projects, and in conversations as we swing together. Alysa, thanks for all you teach me, too.

My colleagues at Lewis & Clark are always ready to hear me go on and on about the wonders of kindergarten literacy. I especially appreciate the patience and listening ear of Kimberly Campbell, who read drafts of this book, Jessie Singer, who was a cheerleader through the process exclaiming over every photo and fieldnote I showed her, and Jill Ostrow, who helped me extend expert tea parties to the world of my graduate students.

Andie and I both thank Brenda as the best editor in the world. But I am even more grateful than that for her solid friendship. When I lose faith in myself or my ideas, I know I can turn to Brenda, my best friend for twenty years.

Jim Whitney's artist eye and technical genius guided us through many challenges as we gathered data and wrote. He spent countless weekends and work nights taking professional photos of student work, and correcting our classroom photos. He served as

computer guru and sounding board, serving up equal helpings of support and off-beat humor. You give me laughter, and inspiration, and love. A thousand thanks.

    Namaste,
    Ruth

Hoose, Phillip, Hannah Hoose, and Debbie Tilley. 1998. *Hey, Little Ant.* Berkeley, CA: Tricycle Press.

Hunter, Ryan Ann. 1999. *Dig a Tunnel.* Illus. by Edward Miller. New York: Holiday House.

James, Simon. 1997. *Leon and Bob.* Cambridge, MA: Candlewick.

Kessler, Leonard. 1999. *Last One in Is a Rotten Egg.* New York: HarperTrophy.

Khan, Rukhsana. 1998. *The Roses in My Carpet.* Illus. by Ronald Humler. New York: Holiday House.

Knowlton, Laurie. 1995. *Why Cowboys Sleep with Their Boots On.* Gretna, LA: Pelican.

Lee, Huy Youn. 1998. *At the Beach.* New York: Henry Holt.

Levens, George. 1999. *Pumpkin Circle: The Story of a Garden.* Photography by Samuel Thaler. Berkeley, CA: Tricycle Press.

Mallet, David. 1997. *Inch by Inch: The Gardening Song.* Illus. by Ora Eitar. New York: HarperTrophy.

McCarty, Peter. 2002. *Hondo and Fabian.* New York: Henry Holt.

McPhail, David. 2000. *Drawing Lessons from a Bear.* Boston: Little, Brown.

Munsch, Robert. 1980. *The Paperbag Princess.* Illus. by Michael Martchenko. New York: Annick.

Nelson, S. D. 2003. *The Star People: A Lakota Story.* New York: Harry N. Abrams.

Nobisso, Josephine. 2002. *In English, of Course.* Illus. by Dasha Ziborova. Westhampton Beach, NY: Gingerbread House.

Nolan, Dennis. 1987. *The Castle Builder.* New York: Simon & Schuster.

Oliver, Mary. 2003. *Owls and Other Fantasies: Poems and Essays.* Boston: Beacon.

Page, Robin, and Steve Jenkins. 2003. *What Do You Do with a Tail Like This?* Boston: Houghton Mifflin.

Plourde, Lynn, and Greg Couch. 1999. *Wild Child.* New York: Simon & Schuster.

———. 2001. *Winter Waits.* New York: Simon & Schuster.

———. 2002. *Spring's Sprung.* New York: Simon & Schuster.

———. 2003. *Summer's Vacation.* New York: Simon & Schuster.

Polacco, Patricia. 1999. *I Can Hear the Sun.* New York: Puffin.

Rathman, Peggy. 1995. *Officer Buckle and Gloria.* New York: Putnam.

Reynolds, Peter. 2003. *The Dot.* Cambridge, MA: Candlewick.

Richmond, Marianne. 2001. *Hooray for You! A Celebration of You-Ness.* Minneapolis, MN: Marianne Richmond Studios.

Romanova, Natalia. 1989. *Once There Was a Tree.* Illus. by Gennady Spirin. New York: Puffin.

Root, Phyllis, and Christoper Denise. 2002. *Oliver Finds His Way.* Cambridge, MA: Candlewick.

Rosenberry, Vera. 2003. *The Growing-up Tree.* New York: Holiday House.

Sadler, Marilyn. 1983. *It's Not Easy Being a Bunny.* New York: Random House.

Soto, Gary. 1993. *Too Many Tamales.* Illus. by Ed Martinez. New York: Putnam.

Stuve-Bodeen, Stephanie. 2003. *Babu's Song.* Illus. by Aaron Boyd. New York: Lee and Low.

Thornhill, Jan. 1997. *Before and After: A Book of Nature Timescapes.* Washington, DC: National Geographic.

Van Allsburg, Chris. 1986. *The Stranger.* Boston: Houghton Mifflin.

Waber, Bernard. 2002. *Courage.* Boston: Walter Lorraine.

Waddell, Martin, and Patrick Benson. 1996. *Owl Babies.* Cambridge, MA: Candlewick.

Walters, Michael, and Harry Taylor. 1994. *Birds' Eggs.* New York: Penguin.

Winer, Yvonne. 2002. *Birds Build Nests.* Watertown, MA: Charlesbridge.

Wood, Douglas. 2001. *A Quiet Place.* Illus. by Dan Andreasen. New York: Simon & Schuster.

Woodson, Jacqueline. 2002. *Visiting Day.* Illus. by James Ransome. New York: Scholastic.

Yolen, Jane. 2003. *Least Things: Poems About Small Natures.* Photographs by Jason Stemple. Honesdale, PA: Boyds Mills.

Professional Literature

Barnhart, Diane, and Vicki Leon. 1994. *Tidepools: The Bright World of the Rocky Shoreline.* Upper Saddle River, NJ: Pearson Educational.

Brosterman, Norman. 1997. *Inventing Kindergarten.* New York: Harry N. Abrams.

Clay, Marie. 2004. Keynote Presentation, "In the Early World," International Reading Association, May 5, 2004, Reno, Nevada.

Gracey, Harry. 1967. "Learning the Student Role: Kindergarten as Academic Bootcamp." In *Sociology of Contemporary Society* 11: 243–254.

Flaherty, Alice. 2004. *The Midnight Disease: The Drive to Write, Writer's Block, and the Creative Brain.* Boston: Houghton Mifflin.

Harvey, Stephanie, and Anne Goudvis. 2000. *Strategies That Work: Teaching Comprehension to Enhance Understanding.* Portland, ME: Stenhouse.

Keene, Ellin, and Susan Zimmermann. 1997. *Mosaic of Thought: Teaching Comprehension in a Reader's Workshop.* Portsmouth, NH: Heinemann.

Miller, Debbie. 2002. *Reading with Meaning: Teaching Comprehension in the Primary Grades.* Portland, ME: Stenhouse.

Palmer, Parker. 1998. *The Courage to Teach.* San Francisco: Jossey-Bass.

Pearson, P. D., L. R. Roehler, J. A. Dole, and G. G. Duffy. 1992. "Developing Expertise in Reading Comprehension." In J. Samuels and A. Farstrup, eds., *What Research Has to Say About Reading Instruction.* Newark, DE: International Reading Association.

Tierney, R. J., and J. W. Cunningham. 1984. "Research in Teaching Reading Comprehension." In P. D. Pearson, ed., *Handbook of Reading Research.* White Plains, NY: Longman.

Tovani, Cris. 2000. *I Read It, but I Don't Get It: Comprehension Strategies for Adolescent Readers.* Portland, ME: Stenhouse.

Starting with Comprehension